Free Money Now!

Find the funds to turn dreams…

to reality

Cynthia Hopper

LEGAL NOTICE

The Publisher and Author have strived to be as accurate and complete as possible in the creation of this book,

Notwithstanding the fact that they do not warrant or represent at any time that the contents within are accurate due to the rapidly changing nature of the Internet and financial laws.

While all attempts have been made to verify information provided in this publication, the Publisher and Author assume no responsibility for errors, omissions, or contrary interpretation of the subject matter herein. Any perceived slights of specific persons, peoples, or organizations are unintentional.

Like anything else in life, no guarantee of income is made. You are advised to use your own wise judgment and due diligence in applying the information within this book to your circumstance and condition.

This book is not intended to be a source of professional, legal, financial and/or accounting advice. Where these subjects are concerned, you are advised to seek competent advice from professionals.

Economically repressed?

This book is for you!

There is a way to sleep well, live in

peace &

Win the financial game!

Cynthia Hopper, is known as Super Cindy Cash Crusader, but it hasn't always been that way.

She was raised in Vienna, Virginia, just outside Washington, DC. Cindy's parents, both successful in real estate, - provided all the trappings that their success suggested: a custom home, new Cadillacs in the driveway, pleasure boating on the weekends – you get the picture.

Cindy believed that was how life was for everyone and she took it all for granted. She had no understanding or appreciation for the lessons that surrounded her.

Just at the time her parents *could* have begun mentoring her in the ways of money and finances, she rebelled. While her peers were going off to college, preparing for careers and adulthood, Cindy took off on her own. Instead of learning about real estate and financial freedom, she learned the lessons of a hard life on the road. By working at low-paying jobs, she seemed to always be left with more month than money.

The old saying proved to be true: Necessity *is* the mother of invention, so Cindy learned how to stretch every dollar. She became obsessed with how to do more with less.

Along the way, she learned how to be frugal and how to use credit to its best possible advantage. After years of practice, Cindy finds "free money," to "play the game . . . and win!" Now, she teaches others how to do the same!

A lot of people have never known the good life. Cindy did, and threw it away.

The take away is this: no matter where we start, we can all end up needing more financial freedom. Through the tough times, Cindy has learned how to use the bank's money and credit to "Beat them at their own game."

This is Cindy's mission: to share what she has learned about winning the game, gaining financial freedom. Now she is passing that wisdom on to you!

She recognizes how our system is often set up to make us fail financially. From credit card nonsense, to opportunities for discounts, to being seduced by our wants instead of our needs. Cindy has lived it, overcome the challenges, and is now your best teacher and mentor.

supercindycc@gmail.com
beatthemattheirowngame.com
Cynthia Hopper@SuperCindyCC

Acknowledgement

Thank you, Barbara Loraine, your encouragement, support, and expertise in all things business proved to be the most important and valuable tool in my toolbox.

This work would not exist were it not for you!

Contents

Free Money Now!

Introduction

> **Cost of Money: The Time Value of Money**
> The time value of money refers to the fact that a dollar in hand is worth more than a dollar at some future time.

According to a 2016 article on money.cnn.com, 76 million Americans struggle financially, either they are just getting by or are they are barely making each month. The American Psychological Association reports that 75 percent of American citizens experience financial stress at least some of the time, and that almost 25 percent say they are under extreme financial stress all the time.

Respondents to one survey said the biggest source of friction and stress in their relationships stem from financial concerns. Couples site money problems as a primary cause of their divorce.

Money impacts every part of our lives.

Many people don't have a plan or foundation that will allow them to effectively deal with their money woes.

I feel it's safe to say that far too many people spend far too much time stressed about and controlled by financial fears.

Wouldn't it be great to not be a slave to money stresses and find a way to deal with, and win the "money game?"

Free Money Now! answers that need.

Free Money Now!'s inspiration came when Cynthia became convinced that her processes would help people avoid frustration, alleviate fears, and fight the destructive, long-term effects that unanswered money matters can have on their lives!

Free Money Now! teaches you not listen to the "experts" when they say that credit is bad, and that using credit is detrimental to your financial health. It is only when we have an uncontrolled, over use of credit that becomes bad. With a specific objective in mind, a well thought out plan in order, and meticulous attention to detail, using credit can not only be safe and good, it can have incredibly awesome results!

It Works!

I know it works because I have been working it for years.

Today I am sitting high and dry under the new roof I had installed just last week using free money I received using the techniques I am about to teach you.

I have found ways to defer paying for nearly everything I buy and every project I undertake. At the same time, I find ways to receive discounts that are often stacked and compounded. I have financed everything from utility bills to housewares to major purchases like the roof I just mentioned using other people's money! In fact, in doing this I have seen my credit scores climb over time. That is beating them at their own game! The pages that follow outline the tips, strategies, and techniques that have taken me years to learn and perfect. In that time, I have grown to know and depend on the fact that this process does work.

I get so excited when I find myself beating them at their own game that I can't wait to tell my friends and anyone else who'll listen how I did it. I bet when you start playing the money game and winning you'll want to tell all your friends and neighbors too!

The strategies in this book have made my life better and easier. I know if you commit to doing these steps you read about in this this program you will reap the same results that I have.

About five years ago, I was in a low spot in my credit journey. There was no way any bank was going to issue me a line of credit. I had low scores on my credit reports. It was the second time in my life that I had ruined my credit and had to start over from less than zero.

I had gotten there by making some terrible decisions and taking some steps that ended up costing me my good credit rating.

With that said, I feel I should acknowledge that many times diligent people who are very careful with their money and don't make stupid decisions find themselves in bad situations. There are times in people's lives when situations are beyond their control and out of our hands. It is unfortunate, but nonetheless true, that bad things do indeed happen to good people. So, if you happen to be one the unfortunate people that are going through divorce, dealing with a medical emergency, or have lost your income you may not have any choice but to let your credit go bad. It is not my intention to make light of the devastation you feel or belittle your circumstance with a flippant, callous attitude.

In these last five years, I have personally taken all the steps that I will show you in this program and can stand before anyone and testify that this process has turned my entire financial life around.

Today I stand on solid financial ground. I am not stressed, worried or afraid. I do not have to screen my phone calls to hide from creditors (although, I do still hide from solicitors!). Now, when I get my credit card statements I am actually eager to read them. In fact, today I got one of my statements in the mail. I opened it immediately to see the good news. My current FICO score was reported to be just shy of 800! I went from disastrous to fabulous in no time at all!

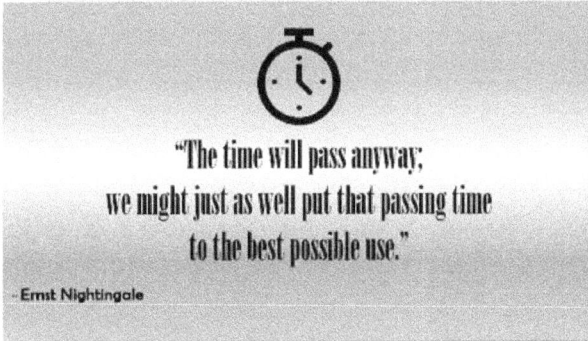

"The time will pass anyway;
we might just as well put that passing time
to the best possible use."

- Ernst Nightingale

I know, I know, I can hear you thinking, "five years. That is not no time!" Well, look at it this way. What else will you be doing for the next several years? You might as well use the time to its fullest and accomplish everything you can. Just add "fixing my numbers" to your to do list. Thankfully, many of you will not be have bad financial problems. If you want to accomplish even better numbers and quickly go from where you are to where you want to be, simply follow this plan. We will discuss your situation (and how to make the most of it) in detail as well. Like I said, this is for everyone!

The biggest thing for me is this; I want other people to have the same kind of success that I have, even with my ridiculously bad history. I am sure that when I pass on what I know I will help people live better lives, happier lives. This is my reward!

I want to shout out to all the world, "You don't have to suffer and be intimidated anymore!".

When you steer clear of financial bondage and land in peace and victory then you can tell everyone you know that you know how to beat them at their own game!

I am certain that you too will have great success. Just follow the steps, be patient and, (this is really important) stay on top of everything you are doing with a great record keeping system.

We will go over how to keep track of all your strategies in the "Staying Organized and on Track" section later in these pages.

It has taken me these last five years, but I come to know for sure that the knowledge I have will help you love your life!

One: Begin Your "Free Money Now!" Journey!

Let's begin with the definition of line of credit (LOC).

A line of credit is a financial product you have that does not have a fixed period in which you must pay it off.

There are three main types of LOC. Allow me to elaborate on the differences and distinctions between the three.

- The first type of a line of credit we will look at is the credit card. Most credit cards can be used for any purpose. They are often associated with high interest rates. Many credit cards today give you some type of reward when you use the card to make a purchase. The rewards I personally find to be the most useful are the cash back rewards. These are a good fit for me, but other people may find that other types of rewards are better for them. Other types of rewards will come as cash credit towards plane tickets, new cars, or merchant specific gift cards. Often the interest-rates on credit cards will be higher than what you will find on the next two types of lines of credit.

Credit cards have been given a bad reputation because many times people do not manage their purchases carefully and they end up carrying large balances form month to month forcing them to pay high interest and then falling behind with their payments.

You will learn how to be in control of your credit life by making educated decisions about what's a good deal and what is not. This program will make *you* the recipient of the "interest" in the form of rewards and incentives. Not the bank. You will see that rewards cards are one important tool in this program. The next two types of lines of credit do not normally offer rewards.

- The second type of line of credit is a signature line of credit. This can differ from a credit card because these have a higher limit than a credit card. Normally they have a lower interest rate than credit cards do. Many people use a signature line of credit for emergencies or to pay off higher interest rate debt. Like that on their credit cards.

- The third type of line of credit is the home equity line of credit. This has the lowest interest-rate because it is secured. What secured means is that if you default on payments the bank has recourse that allows them to take the collateral; Your home! One great use of a home equity line of credit is funding large, costly home improvement projects.

Think about the different ways each of the lines of credit can be use. This can help determine which type you may want to use. Most people will often have a couple of the different lines of credit in place at a time.

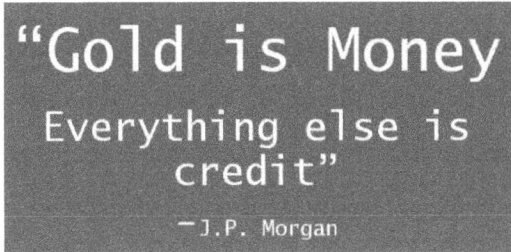

"Gold is Money
Everything else is
credit"
— J.P. Morgan

Section 1 – FREE yourself

If you're like lots of other people you have been conditioned to believe that realizing financial goals only happens for the *other* guy. The good news is that is WRONG! You too can take the steps necessary to make your needs, hopes and dreams become a reality. I have managed to put off paying in full for almost every bill and purchase I make for months and often even years all while continuing to earn interest on my money. I don't mean to imply that you will never pay back what you owe. But Rather, I am saying is that keeping what you have for as long as possible is the best way to handle and grow wealth. This is the subject of this study. I will share with you how I manage to keep my money in my accounts earning interest and growing in value beyond what one would normally expect. The way to do this is to find a way to not use your own funds, but use someone else's to get your stuff done.

Let's spend some time considering ways that you can FREE yourself to new possibilities and great opportunities!

F - Fix your mind

R - Repair mistakes

E - Exalt your profile

E - Elevate your score

F - Fix your mind: You can make the changes needed to reach your goals! It is simple, and anyone can do it. If you are anything like me, you have had to, or still need to, overcome some negative beliefs and thoughts about yourself. These strongholds often begin at an early age and become so ingrained in us that they make success nearly impossible. We look harder at this in a later section.

R - Repair: The term "repair" tends to mean that something is broke. When is the last time you reviewed your credit reports? Your scores could be negatively impacted by wrong information. There are three credit reporting agencies: Equifax, Experian, and Trans Union. Each of these agencies can, and probably will report different information. You must check all three reports for accuracy. Everyone can get free copies of their credit reports from every agency once a year.

There are places you can get a "credit score" at no cost. The score you will find there at these alternative sources are an estimate. I find that the estimate at Credit Karma is a pretty good representation of the actual score and will suffice for the most part. To acquire your reports simply go to freecreditreport.com and fill in the blanks and download and/or print your reports. Once you have accessed your reports review them carefully. Depending on how many years and how many accounts reported this could be an exercise in patience. The good news is that the credit reporting agencies make contesting and fixing discrepancies easy and basically pain free.

Start by going through your credit report and writing down all the different items that you need to dispute.

Disputing incorrect entries is easier than you might expect. Credit rating agencies are legally bound to research each and every single claim of inaccuracy.

Go through the credit report from each reporting agency and note each inaccurate account.

-- Contact the Agencies

The best way to contact an agency is through the mail. Letters of dispute can be tracked using certified mail. Make sure you keep records of every letter you send in case you must take further action in the future.

Mail the agency with a listing of all inaccuracies and request that they either be removed, or they provide proof that the item is correct.

You should receive a response within about 30 days.

Note that sometimes reporting agencies will remove your item in 30 days and put it back in the report if they receive the proof later. If that's the case, they'll need to send you the proof and a letter informing you that the item was placed back on your report.

If you don't get a written notice, you're legally eligible for $1,000 from the reporting agency.

Disputing bad marks is a no-brainer. By taking the time to write these letters and keep track of the dates you can save yourself a lot of grief and aggravation trying to fix bad marks. Many times, this is the only thing you will have to do to get bad marks deleted from your report.

Something that you should consider is the amount of time and energy it takes to go through this process. Simply trying to hold onto and track all the pieces and parts takes a lot of concentration. For many people, it can be stressful.

Should you do it on your own? It depends on whether you'd rather have the time or have the money. If you can spare the time and would rather do it yourself, it's absolutely a viable method and thousands of people do it every year.

Once you have reviewed your reports for errors and negative remarks begin your letter writing campaign and watch your score improve!

With a new, improved score you are increasing the odds of attracting great new offers from credit issuers.

Exalt

verb | ex – alt | \ig – 'zo'lt\
1 : to raise in rank, power, or character
2 : to raise high : ELEVATE

E- Exalt: Depending on your situation improving your credit might be a critical step or something you can gloss over. If you are one of the lucky ones with a score above 600 you are already in the good range and there is really no need to sweat improving your number. That will come naturally when you adhere to the rules listed in the next section, elevate, just follow the elevate guidelines and it will come.

If you would rather not pay for your actual FICO score, go to creditkarma.com for a good representation of what your score looks like. It is an estimate but is good enough for what we are trying to accomplish here. This is a free service.

If your score is below the "good" range you need to do some work in this area, just keep reading. The same steps in elevate will help to improve your numbers. The is a wonderful technicality that you can use to force the reporting agencies to take the offending marks off you reports.

If you are lucky (many people will fall into this category) you will be able to take advantage of the Fair Credit Recording Act's (FCRA) section 609. The loophole allows you to dispute bad marks and have them removed even if they are true (more in the next section **Elevate** about the FCRA section 609).

Otherwise, once the offending item is 7 years old you can request it be removed if it does not automatically fall off.

E - Elevate: Take what you have and work it! Just because your current score looks good doesn't mean you just sit back and do nothing.

There are some simple ways to take your score from good to excellent. The following are a few ways to kick your score up a notch or two! It could mean as much as 60 – 100 points for many people!

1. **Keep your credit utilization at a recommended level or less.**

Your overall usage (credit utilization) should be kept at or below the recommended amount of 30%. So, if the combined amount of credit you have is $10,000 you should keep your total debt at or under $3000. Maxing out your cards will deal a significant blow to your score.

2. **Be aware that older accounts make you more attractive and give your score a boost.**

The longer you have been establishing you credit the better. Lenders are looking for stability and nothing can show how stable you are better that a long history on your report. If you were to close old accounts, even if you don't use them anymore, you are shortening your history. It should be noted that some banks and retailer will close an account after a given period of inactivity. It couldn't hurt to occasionally make a purchase or two with an old card or contact the company to learn what their criteria is for closing inactive accounts.

3. **Debt balance to credit limit ratio**.

Again, the rule of thumb is to keep your balance at 30% or less of your available credit line for each account you possess. It is better to have a couple of accounts active with smaller balances than one account active with a balance over 30% of your available credit line. A great way to combat this is to ask for a limit increase. If your approved your usage percentage will shrinks in comparison effectively lowering your usage percentage.

4. **Make two payments every month.**

The credit companies report balances on accounts one time every month so if you make a payment half way into the month the lower balance is what's reported. That makes your look better and,

That's beating them at their own game!

Now, bear with me as I repeat what I said before. This is, I think, one the easiest solutions to what looks like a complicated problem, so I believe it is worth a second look!

I highly recommend that you fill out a dispute for **all** negative and adverse marks on your credit reports. The Fair Credit Reporting Repair Act section 609, asserts that credit reporting agencies must be able to

Section 609 Credit Restoration Fully Applies the Law

The credit bureaus are regulated by the government due to the nature of their business, but it's important to understand they are private companies. They are NOT legally or morally obligated to report anything on anybody. For example, most people know that most negative events remain on a credit report for seven years (ten years for Chapter 7 bankruptcies). Isn't this a legal requirement? No. They could take all bankruptcies off all records tomorrow, if they chose to. They are simply not allowed by law to report these events for MORE than seven years (or ten). They're not forced to report them at all. Of course, it's their business. That's why they do it. But they have a choice and, when forced to verify the data they report, they will choose to take negative events off. To boil it down, credit restoration doesn't eliminate negative credit events. It does make them in effect "invisible" to anyone looking at a credit report.

produce a document signed by you, the account holder, which states that any negative or adverse accounts are indeed yours. If they cannot produce this document, they have no choice but to remove the negative item from your report. Not only that, the agency has just 30 days to respond to your letter. Remember, if they fail to respond to your letters within the 30 days they must pay you. Now because of the time sensitivity of this you absolutely need to send your letters by certified mail. You will need the stamped date on the letter if you are going to hold the credit reporting agency to the 30-day rule.

You need to be committed to this plan of attack. You will have to be diligent in your letter writing campaign. It may take several months, or it could only take one letter per account. It all just depends on each person's individual circumstances. Don't get discouraged. Just keep plugging along. It is so worth the effort!

Section 2 – What I do

The following is an example of how I used a few of the techniques I employ in this program to undertake a big, expensive project, and keep it pretty much painless!

After receiving yet another rate hike on my home owner's policy I decided it was time to figure out what I needed to do to rope this bill back into line.

I'm always looking for ways to save money so taking on this challenge is something I almost look forward to. Doing whatever it takes to stop the detestable rate creep was well worth the time and effort.

After getting price quote form 3 or 4 inspection agencies, I hired one to go over my home, from top to bottom, and determine where I had problems that could be contributing to the yearly increases in my homeowner's policy.

After going over my report with the inspector it was clear where most of my problem was coming from. The inspection showed me that there was one big issue. My roof was affecting my premiums in a negative way. Even through it was still had a few good years left it was causing my rate creep. At nearly 20 years old the insurance company saw it as an added risk in the event of A hurricane, and they were making me pay for it with a higher rate each passing year. I knew the initial costs of a replacement were going to be high. But I also knew that in the end I would see significant savings in my premiums for many years to come.

. I decided it was time to bite the bullet and go ahead with the upgrades that would address and solve this problem. Even though the initial cost was high I knew that the savings I would see on my insurance premiums in the coming years would help to negate some of the costs, and make this investment more palatable.

I decided to move forward and invest in the needed upgrades.

2017 Insurance Premium	
Before the new roof	$1,270.00
After the new roof	$971.00

That a savings of 23.5% a year for at least 8 more years!

I had been putting off and dreading having a new roof installed for number of years. The job of interviewing contractors to replace the existing structure was not one in which I looked forward to. Now I knew it had to be done and the sooner the better.

> **Crowdsourcing**
> **A specific sourcing model in which individuals or organizations use contributions from Internet users to obtain needed services or ideas. Crowdsourcing was coined in 2005 as a portmanteau *of crowd and outsourcing***

I started by utilizing some of the Web's free referral services. I am talking about sites like Angie's list, Home Advisor, etc. It is also important to note that social media affords great opportunities to use other people's experiences to learn about the good, the bad, and the best service providers in the area. Let social media (or crowed sourcing) do what it does organically; provide valuable insight and ideas.

It's free, and I personally believe, a great way to find good, honest, and reliable service people and contractors. Really, who could be better at giving advice and testimonials about hiring a contractor in your area than your own neighbors?

> ## Education is what you get when you read the fine print. Experience is what you get when you don't. — Pete Seager

There are several crowd sourcing opportunities that are simple to use plus you get the benefit of being introduced to people in *your* community. I have found that the local "Nextdoor" social media sites are a gold mine of honest and relevant opinions. Just post your question and watch the responses roll in!

Section 3 - A roof story

One of my neighborhood Facebook responders told me about a new program that is backed by my county. With this program, homeowners can get energy saving and weather preparedness improvements completed with special financing options. The program is sponsored in select counties in Florida, California, and Texas. It allows homeowners to get work done with no money down and no monthly payments. It boils down to this: an agreed upon payment amount is included as an add-od line on the properties yearly tax document. The homeowner then pays this agreed upon amount along with their property taxes.

The representative from the finance company came to my home to explain how this program worked. He painted a rosy picture of this, and I felt like this was a great way for me to get my new roof. I decided to go for it and utilize the plan to get the work done.

Sounds great, right?

Well, let me say this, the old saying of: "if sounds too good to be true it probably is" proved to be utterly true in this case.

Long story short, when I finally received the actual paperwork (over a week later) I found additional fees and closing costs on the contract that the representative failed to mention. These added costs totaled over $1,200.

I'll be talking more about this and other kinds of offers that are set up to trick and take advantage of people. I call them "the dirty trick men".

The cautionary tale: if I had not made myself tackle the unpleasant job of reading and attempting to understand all the small print included in the finance company's contract the representative (who, I'm sure, was making a big fat commission!) would have, for lack of a better word, *duped* me into paying for all those unmentioned additional fees.

Finally, I ended up financing this project using techniques that I have come to rely on whenever I want to save money. And of course, that is always!

This is what I call winning the game!

Now I will begin taking you through the steps, tips, and techniques that I and anyone else can do to find the funds they need to finance their goals, hopes and dreams. We will explore the many options and opportunities that are available to everyone with just a little legwork, knowledge, and patience.

Here are the details of how I saved on the roof project.

The initial bid for my new roof was: $6,250.00
I got bids from 4 different roofing companies. I made it a point to not hire anyone the day they made their bid. Finally, the best offer of $5,600 came from the fourth company to place a bid. Another advantage was that I actually liked that company the best. They were by far the most professional and they took the time to cover every little detail of my roofing job. He talked about many things that had never occurred to me, like taking pictures down from the walls and putting breakables away. All that hammering and stomping around on the roof causes a lot of rattling and shakes up the contents of the house pretty good! I had to resist the temptation to sign that day.

To create a little tension with the vendors, I decided to wait and see who was the most eager for my business. Fortunately, the waiting initiated a small bidding war between the contractors. After about a week, the first, second and third representatives began calling me trying to get me to commit. At which time I told them I had a better offer form the fourth contractor. They all not only agreed to meet his price, but an even better offer came when one countered his offer at $300 less than the best offer that I had received from my favorite.

I then reached out to my favorite bidder and told him about the other offers. He said he was not going to lose the job for $300. So now I was looking at $5,300. not $6,250! I saw savings of almost $1,000 because I waited.

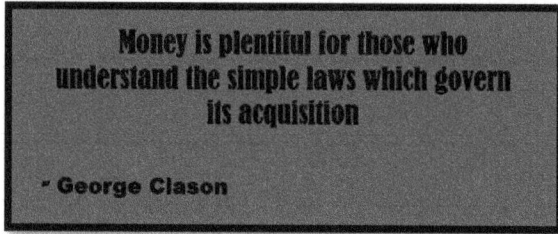

> **Money is plentiful for those who understand the simple laws which govern its acquisition**
>
> ~ **George Clason**

Now that I was confident that I had gotten the best deal possible I hired him on the spot.

I did some number crunching and determined that I wanted to pay for some of the job in cash and then use a convenience check that a bank had sent me. It stated that I could get up to, I think, $7,000 interest free for 18 months. That's a great deal!

Just to be on the safe side I thought I should make sure I knew what I was getting myself into before I used the check to get that $3500, I went in person at the bank and sat down with an associate. The mailer advertised that the money from the check would be interest free for 18 months. True enough, but… as it turns out, somewhere buried down in the small print (which I never did see!) was a dirty trick. In it they disclosed that there was a cash advance fee that was of 2% of the loan amount (so it was $70) and that the interest rate would become retroactive at 23% if the loan was carried past the expiration date of the initial 18 months. I knew exactly how I will deal with this detail when the time comes.

I believe it is unwise to get involved with a loan that could potentially end up resulting in 23% interest *unless* you have an exceptional record keeping system in place that helps you avoid missteps that can make using offers like this a big mistake. And, of course I do. keep great records! I have perfected my record keeping system and I have total confidence in it. It is more than sufficient at keeping me on top of what's happening with my accounts. Because of this I am comfortable taking advantage of these kinds of deals.

Later in chapter *Ten: Staying organized and on track*, I will go into detail about how to set up and keep great records and notifications that will ensure you that you are also going to be able to keep up with everything you have going on in your financial strategy.

The thing I missed with the convenience checks was that by using the convenience checks it was considered a "cash advance". There was a better way to access the available funds on that credit card, which was done through the associate right there at the bank. They just tapped those same funds, but did in a way that it was considered a "direct deposit" instead of a cash advance. Basically, it all came down to how the funds were accessed! By obtaining the money as a "direct deposit" the terms were much better: A 2% fee and normal interest rate after the 18 months. The initial impression I had was that when I used a check to get the money it would be handled like a normal balance transfer. I was wrong. Now I hate to be a negative Nelly, but I believe that they intentionally made some of the sketchier details of those "convenience checks" confusing and even hard to see so that we will not understand or even notice them until it is too late, and we have taken the bait.

The Banker says: "I want *your* money now!"

You say: "I want *free* money now!"

Okay, so now I have financed my roof job. I only spent $1800 of my own money. The balance of $3500 is now financed for 18 months at 0 percent interest, which allows my $3500 to stay put in a money market, IRA or CD growing in value every day! By the time the 18 months is up, that $3500 I still have sitting in my name will have probably grown from anywhere around 6% to as much as 15% depending on the economy and the market. We have all heard about how

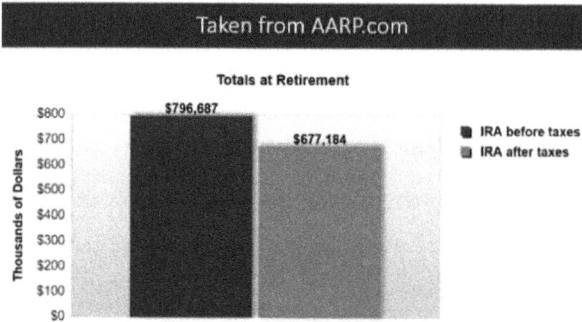

the growth of Individual Retirement Accounts (IRA) grows exponentially when we leave it alone for years to come. By using other people's money to do your big projects you may be able to avoid pulling funds out of your IRA, avoiding the tax penalties, and setting yourself up for greater growth.

By the way, when the 18 months is up, and my interest free offer expires I will move the remaining balance to another, different interest free offer. I know that if I keep up with my payments my scores will look great. When my scores look great, l will continue to receive these kinds of offers nearly weekly from different banks. That makes this process very easy to do.

There you have it! I am earning interest and growing my funds from the bank while using their money to finance my project! They are not getting interest from me!

Now, that's beating them at their own game!

Two: Personal Profile Matters

Begin with the end in mind

-Steven Covey

Steven Covey wrote in "7 Habits of Highly Successful People" that we should begin every project with the desired end result in mind.

For this project, the desired end result is for you to gain the ability to access and use other people's money to finance projects and delay payment for every day expenses, goals and special projects. All interest free, of course! When you successfully put off payment you get to keep your money in your accounts where they can continue to grow from interest and other gains you are winning at the game of money. When you use your rewards cards, you will even be making money on the funds you borrow. Isn't that just fabulous?! I get so excited when I get the chance to share these tips and techniques with people I can't even describe it!

Now, we will explore what you need to do to get into a position where you can start to take advantage of interest free credit offers.

First things first!

I believe that you must understand exactly where you are now to properly navigate to where you want to be.

Let's begin this journey by taking a good look at your foundation. This is what I refer to as your personal profile. Your personal profile means your current statistics:

- Where you are employed
- Amount of income
- Where you live and how long you have lived there
- Any other relevant financial support
- Types and number of checking/savings accounts you have
- How much debt you currently carry.
- And finally, the big one. What does your FICO (credit scores calculated with software from Fair Isaac Corporation) score and Equifax, Experian and Trans Union, credit reports reveal about you?

I will go into further detail about FICO scores, credit reports and what to do to improve upon them in the next section.

For now, we will look at the "who" and the "what" of a credit score. Lenders do consider all these profile factors when determining the terms of an offer. So, the better your statistics are the better the offers will be. It is important that applicants appear to be stable. Having the same address for a year or longer, having employment that is not brand new, reporting a livable income and having established checking and savings accounts are all pluses in that they add evidence of stability to your profile.

If this describes your situation, great! You are ready to jump right in and start

It is better to have a hen tomorrow that an egg today
- Thomas Fuller

managing accounts and making deals. If not, there are some things you can do to make yourself more attractive to lenders. The positive side is, it is not hard, the negative side is, sometimes nothing but the passage of time will help you get in the best position to start working the system. If you fall into the second category mentioned above, one thing to remember is that most of the time creditors basically rely on the information that *you* supply on your application. Rarely do they put much effort into verifying your information.

Let me say this, you will probably see, for the most part, that decisions are based on the contents of your credit reports and your score. The information on your applications is the information you give. They take the information you give them about length of residency and time on your current employment to determine whether you are stable. Just be aware that you are in control of what is written on the lines of your applications. Keep in mind that not-so-good answers could complicate matters and slow you down.

Now about that one negative. The only way to solve the problem of a short credit history that is too short is to make it longer. The only way to make it longer is by practicing patients while allowing the passage of time.

You must simply wait it out.

When I began the journey of fixing my credit, I was not excited about starting the process all over again. Because this was my second time around I knew it just takes time. My situation would get better when I got down to it and did the work. I just had to jump right in and start taking the baby steps that would eventually lead me to my destination.

I heard a couple of sayings some years ago that have always stuck with me. I pull them out of my mental box of positive self-talk and repeat them anytime I feel like what's in front of me is too much work and I just want to give up. It always helps to keep me motivated and moving forward.

"We do the things we have to do,

so, we can do the things we want to do."

&

"If it's hard, do it hard!" (as motivator, Les Brown says).

I know I am not he only one who has at one time or another, looked at their situation and thought it is just hopeless and fixing it was just going to be too much work. You may think to yourself that it can't and won't be accomplished. I understand that it is easy to feel overwhelmed at these times, but remember that we are never alone. There are countless others who are going through the same thing.

Just continue to push forward and the day **will** come when you see the fruit of all your labor!

Three: Your Score, The Truth and Nothing but The Truth!

> **In times past, your social security number was the most influential number known to man... However, there is a three-digit number that is giving the social security number a run for its money...**
>
> -Cornelius J.
> The Credit Repair Book: The Credit Repair Companies "Secret Weapon"

About Credit Scores

Section 1: Credit Score –What Is It?

Are you in need of a loan, but you have been told that your credit score wasn't high enough? Aren't sure what a credit score is? A credit score is the credit rating that represents your credit worthiness. A complicated statistical model is used to calculate it.

Where does your credit score come from?

Your credit score is normally based on information that can be found in your credit report. Banks and credit card companies use this score to determine the risk they take when lending you money or by extending you credit. Loan processors use your credit score to determine the likelihood of you paying back your loan or failing to repay it over an estimated period.

A few examples of the things lender use your credit score to determine are:

- if you are credit worthy.

- what your interest rate will be.

- what your limits will be.

The most widely used credit score in the United States is the FICO score.

FICO stands for Fair Isaac Corporation. This company developed the mathematical formula that is used to calculate your credit score. This score is one of the most important factors in determining your credit worthiness in the United States. How do you know if your credit score is good enough? You can access your credit scores online at the FICO website. Normally it would cost you about $45 to access this information, but we will be covering some ways for you to get it for less or even free. No matter how you get it you will be thankful you did. You'll be ahead of the game by knowing and understanding this information before you apply for any loan.

If you have ever applied for a loan, you already know how important your credit score is. When a lender looks at your credit score, they decide on how desirable a candidate you are for that loan. Many people don't realize is that we are constantly contributing to our credit scores. Positively or negatively. Paying your bills on time has a positive impact on your score whereas late and missed payments can be crippling to your credit score.

Your credit score is a number ranging from 300 to 900. This number provides potential lenders with important information. A good credit score means that you have made prompt, timely loan payments and have a solid credit history. A low credit score is usually indicative of the fact that you may not honor your financial commitments in a timely manner or could just be that you are new to the credit game.

It's easy to find out your credit score. According to federal law,

Be aware that are many different sources that lenders use in decision making. To confuse matters even more, each source will generate a different score with a different meaning. A few sources are: Vantage, FICO and Beacon

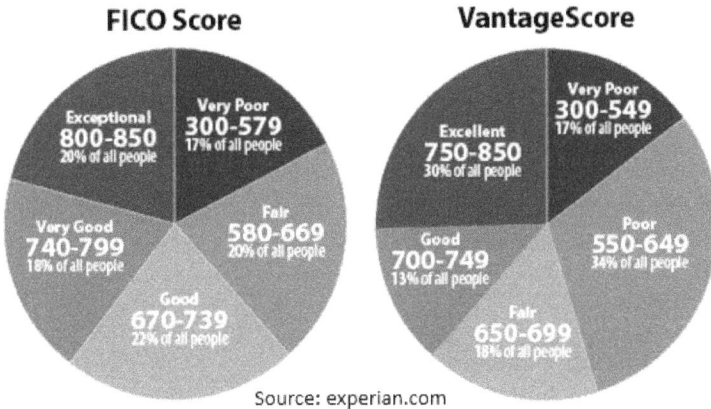

FICO Score

- **Exceptional** 800-850 20% of all people
- **Very Poor** 300-579 17% of all people
- **Fair** 580-669 20% of all people
- **Very Good** 740-799 18% of all people
- **Good** 670-739 22% of all people

VantageScore

- **Excellent** 750-850 30% of all people
- **Very Poor** 300-549 17% of all people
- **Poor** 550-649 34% of all people
- **Good** 700-749 13% of all people
- **Fair** 650-699 18% of all people

Source: experian.com

consumers are entitled to a free credit report each year from each of the 3 credit reporting agencies: Equifax, Experian, and TransUnion. You can then see your credit score. A credit score lower than 600 means you most likely must take some extra measures to secure loans of credit cards. Don't worry! It is still possible for you to begin winning at this credit game. Just stick with me and I will cover what to do further on. myFico.com is the home of the most influential credit score in the U.S.; your FICO score. You can buy a copy of your reports at the sites I have mentioned here before that you can get them for a little as around $15. That is, if you are not entitled to your once yearly free copy.

Here ARE a few ways to get your FICO score for free:

1 Discover Bank

Visit Discover Bank's *Credit Scorecard* program and sign up online. The scorecard website states: "There is no coast or ding to your credit. You don't have to e a customer, and we will never sell your information.

2 Credit cards

Some financial institutions offer their card holders a look at their FICO for free.

Examples include:

- American Express
- Bank of America
- Barclaycard
- Chase Slate
- Citi
- Wells Fargo

3 Auto loans

When financing through certain companies, such as the following, buyers can see their score for free:

- Ally Financial
- Hyundai Capital America

4 Credit Unions

Some credit unions give their members free access to FICO scores. Among these are:

- Pentagon Federal Credit Union
- North Carolina State Employees' Credit Union
- Digital Federal Credit Union
- Pennsylvania State Employees' Credit Union

5 Student Loans

Borrowers and co-signers of Sallie Mae Option undergraduate student loans can see their FICO scores quarterly.

-

6 Credit Counselors

Clients of consumer credit counseling services are entitled to receive their FICO scores for free, according to Consumer reports.

Offering credit scores enables credit consolers to better help their clients improve their financial situations.

Who Checks Your Credit Score?

Like I mentioned before, having a good credit score not only affects your ability to get a loan it also can affect your ability to rent or lease a vehicle, to rent a house or apartment and even, in some instances, your score may even influence your ability to land a job.

Credit card providers check your credit score whenever you apply. Even when you apply for a secured credit your credit could be checked.

While reviewing a credit report is a common practice of businesses in the business of financing, what fewer people realize is that a credit check can be performed to determine one's eligibility for a job or that a prospective landlord can check one's credit score to predict the likelihood that they will be a reliable tenant. In fact, landlords have been known to decline tenants that have a poor credit rating. Further, in terms of home mortgages, one's credit score can even affect the interest rate one receives. Lenders will check credit reports and even if a person is deemed credit worthy, a marginal credit score can earn a person a higher interest rate over the individual that has an excellent credit score.

Section 2: How important is your credit score?

You are judged by your score. What is more important than that? I think, not much! Lenders and other people use this information when deciding if you are a good credit risk.

Your credit score is so important that without a healthy one you may find it hard to get credit cards, a loan for a new car or a mortgage. Your credit score can affect the ability to rent an apartment, get a job and more.

Often, people with poor credit are forced to take loans, mortgages, and credit cards with high interest rates, as these are the only things lenders will allow them to have. Unfortunately, because the interest rates are so high people often find it difficult to meet the repayments. If they can't make the repayments their credit score will dip even further. It's a vicious cycle. Therefore, it is vital that you don't bite off more debt that you can handle. Especially when you are working to get established. The best advice I can offer to people with a poor credit score is this: make sure that you only take credit if you know that you will be able to make the repayments. Once you borrow an amount that you are sure you can afford to repay and it's a good idea to set up automatic payments. That way you can't forget to make your payments on time, every time. You will see that score gradually improve, allowing you to get better financing offers with lower interest rates in the soon.

How Your Credit Score Affects You

If you have ever tried to buy anything on credit or get a loan, then you know that your past credit history will affect the decision the lender makes. If you pay your accounts on time it will be reflected as a good rating on your credit report. If you have missed or MADE late payments it will be reflected as a poor rating on your credit report. Better ratings mean higher scores. The higher your score, the lower interest rates you will get (sometimes even zero percent!) and you will not have any problems receiving lines of credit. The lower the score, the higher your interest rates will be and the harder it will be to get line of credit.

Get your credit score now so you can see what needs to be done to fix it, should you need to. You will be glad you took care of anything that needs it now, rather than later when you need a loan and can't get it. Your credit score does affect you greatly!

Credit Scores and Banks

What is a healthy credit score? What is the connection between your credit score and the banks?

Simply put, your credit score is the primary information used by banks in deciding whether it's worth the risk to lend you money. After all, that's what banks do when they offer you a loan (or a credit card). They gamble on whether you will be able to repay their money. If you pay back the money on time (with a little interest on top) the banks have won the game and their gamble. If you default on a loan (or credit card) and the bank must take you to court or pay a collection agency to recover their money, they have lost their bet and you have a mess on your hands. It's as simple as that.

In the pages that follow we will look at another, third dimension to this credit, interest game. The zero-interest offer. For now, let's continue the discussion about credit scores.

So how do the banks get hold of your credit score? Banks and other lenders purchase your credit report from the credit bureaus that make them. Every time you apply for a loan, take a credit card, open a new bank account, or do any number of things related to finance, the bank will look at your credit report to assess your ability to repay.

Because of all this, it is vital that you make sure you can repay any money you have borrowed – in full and on time. In-full can have different meaning depending on the circumstances surrounding the loan.

Sometimes when I say in-full it means at least your minimum payment, other times it will mean the total balance amount. Regardless, if you find yourself falling behind in your repayments it will affect your credit score, and the next time a bank looks at your credit report they might decide that you're not worth the gamble.

Credit Score Details Online

Your credit score is your credit rating calculated based on several factors. You can find your credit score details online as well as through your bank, local credit bureaus or other credit report companies. Your credit rating is important for so many reasons that you should check your credit score regularly by getting your credit reports. You can easily get your credit score and credit reports online through various websites. Simply type in "credit score," "credit rating" or "credit report" into your favorite search engine and you will see endless websites you can visit that will give you information about credit rating and ways to access your credit score details online.

Some sites will offer instant credit reports; others will claim to have free credit reports. Some have extra features, such as continuous monitoring of your credit score details online as it changes, and the ability to protect yourself against identity theft. Some also offer various package deals, typically monthly.

Important!

Do your research before you choose where to get your credit score. Not all credit report sites are reputable. Get your hands on the credit reporting sites' background information first. It's also a good idea to look at reviews from people who have gone before you. A less costly mistake (like a poor representation of your score) is an inconvenience and misleads but a worse mistake could cost you a lot. Some of these sites will trick you into unwittingly signing up for a monthly service. Then, they begin charging you every month for a service you did not want. If you're not carefully reviewing your bank statements every month this could go on for a long time before you catch it. This happened to my mother, she didn't notice it for about a year. These people had been charging her $30 every month! She definitely could have spent that $360 better! That is losing the game!

Visit Equifax.com, myFICO.com. Experian and TransUnion for your reports

Section 3: Questioning Your Credit Score

Today more than ever, questioning your credit score is an essential practice. Identity theft is on the rise and when you make a standard practice of questioning your credit score you are engaging in one of the critical steps required in protecting your identity. Whether you purchase products and services online or you have ever had a credit card stolen, whether you use the Internet on a regular basis or not, you should **always** question your credit score rating at least one time a year.

Along with the ways we have already discussed to access your credit score there are several other ways. First, if you have recently applied for credit and have

NO WAY!

been denied for any reason, you will receive a letter providing you with a reason for the denial and instructions on how to get your credit report information. Don't throw the denial in the trash. Take advantage of the opportunity to view your credit report. Follow the instructions to get your credit report and find out what creditors are saying about you. You may be surprised by unusual transactions or other wrong information on your report that can be having a negative impact on your credit score. You can also sign up with professional companies to access your credit report from the three main credit bureaus: Experian, Transunion, and Equifax. If while questioning your credit score you find that someone is using your personal information to make purchases, you will need to contact the credit reporting agencies to dispute the reports. You may also be required to contact the reporting creditor to make them aware of the fraudulent activity. In the end, by checking your credit report for critical errors, you can put a fast end to the theft of your identity.

I experienced identity theft when someone filed a fraudulent tax return in my name. It took months to straighten out and required that I get local law enforcement involved, and of course, the IRS. The bad news is that this is increasingly more common. The good news is, because it is so common the authorities know exactly what do to do and will be able to help you get the mess straightened out

Keeping a Good Score Good.

You've been working hard at raising your poor credit rating. Now that you've established good credit, keep it good. Keeping your score in the good range is relatively simple and straightforward. Just use common sense and follow a few guidelines.

Pay your bills as soon as they are due, if not before. It's generally a good rule of thumb to pay more than the minimum payment each month. Keeping a good credit score also involves understanding the exact terms and conditions and making sure your understanding matches that of vendors and creditors. If you're unsure about anything, call them up and get the clarification you need.

If at some point you realize you can't meet your obligation, have a conversation with the lender. It's best to be up-front and honest Never try to dodge and hide. Avoiding the lender will not work and you might effectively cut out some good payment options that may have otherwise been offered to you. Negotiate something with the lender that you know you can manage. Then it's doubly important to follow through and meet the new expectations for keeping your good credit score.

Other important tips for keeping a good credit score include:

- keeping and maintaining a manageable monthly budget
- maintain a steady performance of spending and saving.

If you do these things, keeping your good credit isn't difficult. All the effort you put into this is will prove to be beneficial in a myriad of ways in the future!

Other Factors and Concerns.

Your credit score is not the only thing that determines your credit worthiness. Another factor to consider is your debt to income ratio. Secondly, your personal profile statistics. Of all these are foundational matters. Your score is the one that weighs most heavily on an underwriters' decision-making process and your future opportunities. In most scenarios having at least a score of good (around 700) will keep creditors from scrutinizing your other profile matters (the application) too heavily. Exceptions to this rule would be, for example, when applying for a mortgage. We are not concerned with this type of loan and the resulting deep scrutiny as it is beyond the scope of this project.

Section 4: Credit repair agencies

What to Look for in an agency.

If you happen to be one the millions of Americans that are an unlucky victim of identity theft this could be a viable solution to a complicated problem. They can help you untangle the mess that identity thieves leave in their wake. They can also provide you with valuable advice on ways to fix other issues that you may not feel comfortable handling on your own. There is no shame in asking for help when you need it.

The most important tool against bad credit repair deals is your credit repair contract. Before you sign any kind of contract with a credit repair agency, you need to make sure you're protected.

Most contracts are written by the credit repair agency and are naturally written more for their benefit than yours. That said, if you know what to look for, you can make sure that everything you need is covered in the contract.

Here are the most important clauses to look for in any credit repair contract.

What they are agreeing to do

The contract should explicitly state exactly what the credit repair agency will do for you.

For example, they might commit to sending X letters to X agencies to help you remove items from your report. They might agree to follow up with those companies, as well as to advise you on lawsuit opportunities. If you are also having them take on the task of debt consolidation, make sure you cover all your bases there too. The agreement should spell out explicitly how the consolidation process is handled and what kind of support you'll have during the process.

The Cost Structure

The contract should contain details on how the program is priced. Any implied verbal guarantees should be written into the paperwork. There should be no additional costs that you don't understand, no fine print with extra fees.

Different credit repair agencies charge differently. Some require an upfront fee, others don't. Some charge a percentage of debt, others charge a flat fee.

If you're just having the repair agency remove items from your credit report the usual payment will be made in the form of a "per item" fee. For example, an agency might charge $250 for each item they can remove from a credit report.

Make sure you understand the cost structure and any additional costs before signing the paperwork.

How Long before You Can Expect Results

The contract should have a set duration. Six months to one year is a good time range for an extensive credit repair project. If a contract doesn't have a set duration, make sure you have a clear cancellation period. After all, if you've seen no results for six months, you'll want to make sure you can back out of the deal and find someone else to help you.

Before you sign anything, make sure you read over every line and fully comprehend everything you're signing. If the contract accurately represents everything that you talked about verbally and you believe it's a good deal for you, then sign the paperwork.

According to consumersadvocate.org these are some of the best Credit Repair Agencies for people who live in Florida for the year 2017.

For information on the best agencies in your state go to their website and chose your state. They will give a list of the best agencies in your area.

Four: Fix Your Mind – You Can Win the Money Game!

First, let me provide a short explanation as to why I am telling you the following story. My hope is that I will be able to paint a clearer picture of what I mean when I talk about how our belief systems and self-talk can really mess up our world. My stinking thinking and bad habits went unchecked for decades and nearly ruined my life. It is only through hard work and faith that I managed to turn things around. I am convinced that I would not be the happy, content person I am today had I not attacked these beliefs and fixed my mind.

My story:

At the age of fourteen I decided that I was would be happier taking off and living on the run than I would be staying at home with my parents. Looking back on those days I must admit I still don't fully understand why I traded my privileged life at home for life on the street. I only know that I had convinced myself to do it. It was not an easy existence and I struggled every day just to get by.

I recall that one night being so cold that I sought out refuge in a 24-hour laundromat. I actually tried to sleep in one of those giant dryers. You've probably seen them. They hold about 3 extra-large loads of laundry. I remember that it was impossible to get comfortable because the ribs inside the dryer kept digging into me. I spent the night going form the table people used for folding clothes to curling up in the dryer so no one would see me. For some reason, it seemed reasonable to me to do this. It also seemed okay to get my wardrobe off clothes lines in people's back yards, and that holding up in public restrooms to take a bird bath were all acceptable tradeoffs to life at home. It's amazing what a fourteen your old will endure to prove they are right!

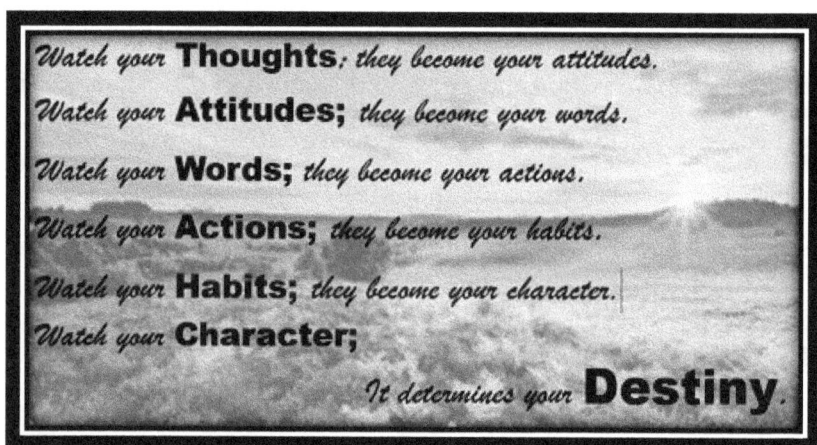

Watch your **Thoughts**; *they become your attitudes.*
Watch your **Attitudes**; *they become your words.*
Watch your **Words**; *they become your actions.*
Watch your **Actions**; *they become your habits.*
Watch your **Habits**; *they become your character.*
Watch your **Character**;
It determines your **Destiny**.

Finally, there came a time that I was so worn out and weary from the nightmares of life on the street. I was absolutely positive, without *any* doubt in my mind, that there was no way I was ever going to do anything that crazy and stupid ever again. I was done suffering.

At least that's what I thought at the time. Again later, when I was at an age when I should have been wiser I picked up some old bad habits again. I did everything exactly as I pleased without any regard for the consequences. I had forgotten the lessons I learned as a teenager.

My life went out of control and my situation only got worse as I tried one ridiculous scheme after another trying to dig myself out of the economic pit I found myself in.

Ultimately, this sequence of events pushed my life into complete failure. Hitting rock bottom forced me to open MY eyes and accept what I had done. I became determined to get it together. There was only one direction left to go, and that was up!

Through this experience, I learned that I had so many wrong beliefs about who and what I was, and what I can achieve. The thoughts that had sabotaged my existence for so long had to go!

I decided I would do the work, no matter how hard, to right my wrongs and make my life count!

This was the catalyst that began my new way of thinking. So, after some serious soul-searching, I spent countless hours reading motivational books, listening to success stories, and seeking out every kind of positive influence I could get my hands on.

Steven Covey's book "7 habits of highly successful people" became my life map. The Holy Bible became my best friend. Eventually all my efforts began to produce fruit.

I came to understand that there really was nothing holding me back except me. I learned that we are what we believe, and no one can determine these beliefs for us but us.

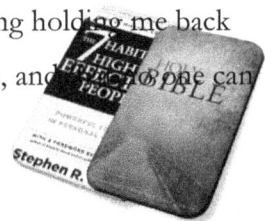

We must set our minds on the truth; that we are the most powerful influence in our own lives and we must never allow anyone to interfere and take that away from us.

If a relationship proves to be a cancer, cut it by out by cutting them out!

So, my questions to you are:

- What do you believe you are worthy of and why do you believe that?

- Do you see yourself as an amazing person who is already a winner just because you are you?

- Can you visualize your life in a place where you can have and do the things you want?

- Do you believe that success is for everyone, including you?

- Are there people in your life that are bringing you down, holding you back and basically raining on your parade?

- What things could you be telling yourself that will boost your self-worth as it stands today?

By taking an honest, critical look at ourselves and the environment we have created, we can begin to fix the things that need to be fixed. Then we can free our minds and become open to change, growth, and power! That's how we begin to beat them at their own game!

Five: Building Your Credit Portfolio

(For those with Poor to Fair numbers)

> ### "The best person to "face" the problem is also the best person to "fix" the problem – that is you!!!
>
> ~Cornelius J.
> The Credit Repair Book: The Credit Repair Companies "Secret Weapon"

Now that you have collected your reports and scores and taken the proper steps to correct any errors or bad information your homework is behind you. It is now time for you to begin putting all of it to work. We will concentrate on you building or rebuilding your credit by opening new accounts to create a fresh, more attractive credit profile. Your numbers will go up and a world of opportunities will open for you

It Is Possible to Repair Bad Credit on Your Own.

Often time's people feel as if they have no choice but to either wait for their credit to improve on its own, or seek professional help. But it is possible to do it yourself.

Not only can you do it yourself, it's often better for your credit for you to do it yourself than to get professional help.

A professional might charge you $200 an item to get it off your credit report. From all three reporting agencies, that's $600 per item! If you instead applied that $600 to paying down a high balance account, you would be further improving your credit. Doesn't that make a lot more sense?

I must say that my expertise in credit rebuilding happened completely by accident. Because I had my own personal credit melt downs in the past I went through these steps and can tell you from experience that they do work. I never sought outside help and I never filed bankruptcy. I learned that if I just waited long enough all the bad stuff just disappeared off my report. Seven years is the period for negative marks to come off your report. But, there are a couple of problems with not filing for bankruptcy. Firstly, I found that by not going through the bankruptcy process creditors haunted me. I just let my answering machine screen my calls and grit my teeth to get through it, and years later a collector can come after your pay check, bank accounts and even your personal property.

If the collectors know where your bank accounts are held they can go through the courts and do what is called "whit of garnishment" where your accounts are frozen. If they find your employer, they can force your bosses to garnish your paycheck up to 25%! You could also have a lean placed on your personal property. These actions are not necessarily the norm, but they are definitely something you should think about. Oh, one more thing, the option for your creditors to do this *never* expires, so beware!

As I said before I had two very serious missteps in my past that created my own credit disasters. Even with those missteps in my history once I started to get my act together by doing some of the things in this chapter my credit started to look better. Retailers, banks, and finance companies solicited me. They all wanted Me! Funny thing is, that's exactly how I got into those messes to begin with! It's true that the more credit you have they more they want to give you. I digress! Let me get back to this discussion!

When financial institutions have little risk, and believe that you will use their card to run up large balances they can't wait to get you signed up. They know those large balances pay them big. They get to keep all the interest you paid. It's a win for the bank and a big fat loss for you.

If you have a low score, either because you have little to no credit or you have made some mistakes in the past there are still some great options for you to employ to quickly get on the road to financial success.

We are going to investigate options that are available to you then you can use them to get you on your way.

How to Handle Your First Credit Card

Good credit is something that has to be worked at and maintained. While, it is difficult to rebuild good credit after financial stumbles, good credit from the start can be maintained much easier. When you turn eighteen you will notice a barrage of credit card and other loan offers coming in the mail, calling you on the phone and popping up in your email. While, some may be tempting with high limits and promises of low interest rates and payments, these can be the traps that walk you straight into large amount of suffocating credit card debt in the future.

To navigate through these offers, you should open them all and read ALL the information carefully. It's important to understand the information included with the offer. While, they may be offering you some enticing offer, the fine print will sometimes reveal that the promotion is only for a short period of time or through certain

restrictions. To help you decide which offers to pitch, which to keep and how to protect yourself from being overwhelmed by the number of offers, follow these tips.

1. Read the fine print.

The fine print will often reveal loopholes in promotions, time restrictions on your initial agreement and other nasty little things, like fees for a variety of things. Other negative surprises could jump out at you later down the line. If there is anything you are uncertain about or you find a company you are not familiar with, take the time to check them out with a site like ZapData or through the Better Business Bureau for complaints and in-depth information.

2. Consider the offers carefully to choose the right one for you.

Before you fill out, call, or send off the credit card applications, choose those that best fit your needs. This doesn't mean you should automatically pick the highest limit or lowest interest rate. As far interest rates, look for stability. Since you are in the process of building or repairing your credit you should probably move with a more cautious hand than someone that already has good numbers. If you are considering two different cards companies and one offers 0% interest for the first three months, then the rate goes to 28%, is it really better than a card that offers 8% interest and never changes?

Of course, the ability to handle more complex terms will vary from one person to the next. So, all I am saying is that if you have any doubts that an offer like this will work for you, don't do it. You want consistency and no nasty surprises. As for the limit, picking the highest limit can be tempting. Just make sure that you don't max out and over spend, just because it's there. Instead, choose a card that offers you a limit to help you in for an emergency situation, or just be enough to meet your goal of boosting your position.

3.Opt-out of future offers

If you feel that getting more offers is going to more temptation than you can handle, then you should opt-out of future offers. The more offers you get and *apply* to the more your credit will be checked. This is harmful to your credit score. There should be opt-out information on the application form itself, sometimes it won't be readily seen, and you will have to look for it a little. There are organizations and sites that can help you opt-out of credit card offers without taking the time to contact each company separately. Check out donotmail.org or optoutprescreen.com for more information and to sign up.

4.Set some rules.

When you first get a credit card, it will seemingly burn a hole in your pocket. You will think about it all the time and you will feel as if you have been given free money, especially if you live on a budget or fixed income and don't often have money for extras. So, it is critical that you set some rules for yourself. Follow these rules and avoid too much credit card debt. You should always try to pay well over the minimum amount. If you charge $1000 and only pay the minimum's, at an average interest rate it would take you at least eight years to pay off the balance. Credit cards can offer an emergency support system that you can fall back on in a time of financial hardship, but if not handled correctly can turn bad and land you in credit card debt that can be difficult to get out of and create a real mess that takes lots of time and energy to correct. It's just easier to be extra careful from the beginning and not have to deal with all that.

Let's look at secured credit cards.

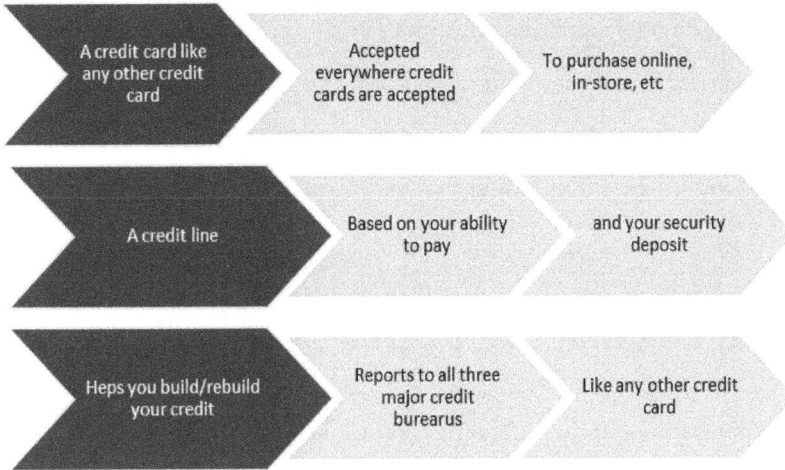

A credit card like any other credit card	Accepted everywhere credit cards are accepted	To purchase online, in-store, etc
A credit line	Based on your ability to pay	and your security deposit
Heps you build/rebuild your credit	Reports to all three major credit burearus	Like any other credit card

An option for those who have trouble getting approved for an unsecured card is a secured card. Secured cards can be used anywhere credit cards are accepted. Most of the time secured cards are reported just like any other account to the credit reporting agencies, so no one will be aware that it is a secured account. Some secured cards come with the option of upgrading to unsecured status. If your card does not have this option, you would simply apply to an unsecured account after some time has passed. Unfortunately, many secured cards do have annual fees, but you shouldn't ever pay more than $50. If you look hard enough you might find secured cards with $0 annual fees. The bottom line: If you can't qualify for an unsecured card, a secured card can be a great tool as you look to improve your credit. And finally, you should know that when you close your secured account, your security deposit is refunded.

Secured cards are obtained by providing monetary collateral in exchange for a credit line. For example, if you make a deposit of $300. You can then charge up to the $300. Then you make payments to the bank just like with any other card. This deposit takes the risk away for the bank. If you don't make your payments they just get the money from your deposit. It allows you to start building your credit and showing that you're creditworthy without someone having to take a financial risk.

- Unlike credit cards which make money on interest, secured cards make most of their money with fees. They'll still charge an interest on the balance, but primarily they make their money from the annual fees.

- Different banks charge different fees. Make sure you fully understand the fees before you sign the agreement.

- Many banks and credit unions offer secured credit cards. Some traditional banks are moving away from secured cards, but many of them still offer this service.

- If you can't find one in person, you can always apply for a secured card online. If you do, make sure to carefully research any company you work with first.

- Do a search on online websites at the BBB and at RipOffReport as there are unscrupulous financial websites out there.

Some final tips:

- Make sure you ask your lending company whether they report the card as a secured card. Some companies do, while others don't. If they don't, move on. It's not going to help you unless it is reported.

Also ask if there will be any indication that the card is secured. Having your card appear as an unsecured card on your credit report will look better than if you had a secured card.

- Make sure you keep a balance on the card and that you make on-time payments every month, even if your balance is just $20. The goal is to build a history of on-time payments and stable accounts.

Now let's talk about store cards.

Store cards many interest rates card because they are Even with the times have higher than their major bank counterparts. That is generally easier to get. higher interest rate this is one of the times when carrying a small balance from one month to the next is a good idea.

This is how you build that history that is so desirable. It is good for your numbers to show a history of on-time payments. The longer the history the better. So, go ahead and plan to pay that interest. A couple of things to keep in mind is your rate of utilization and interest rate. To address these issues, you should keep your balance low. Remember that utilization under 30 percent is desirable. These types of cards often have small limits. You don't want to run your card up to the limit. That hurts your rating. The limits are often around $300, so you would want to keep your balance at or near $100 This works for that higher interest rate as well. After all, wouldn't you rather be paying interest on a $75 balance than that of a $300. balance?

Store cards have an average APR of 23.23 percent, which is about 8 percent higher than a general credit card

Low limits and other factors on these cards can ding your credit score significantly

Photo by Hunter Johnson on Unsplash

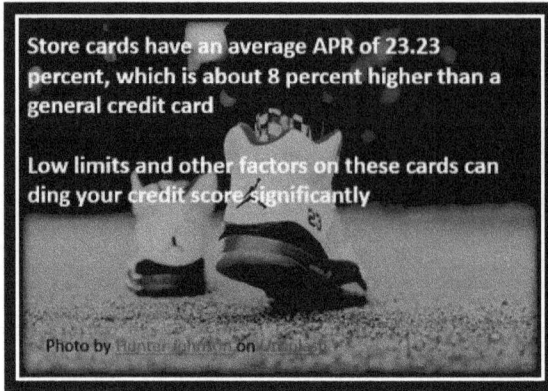

So, go ahead and get that card from your favorite store. Just make sure to spread your purchases out over months. That way you get the benefit of on-time payments while keeping the interest paid and your utilization at a minimum. Another plus is now you have a legitimate reason for more shopping trips!

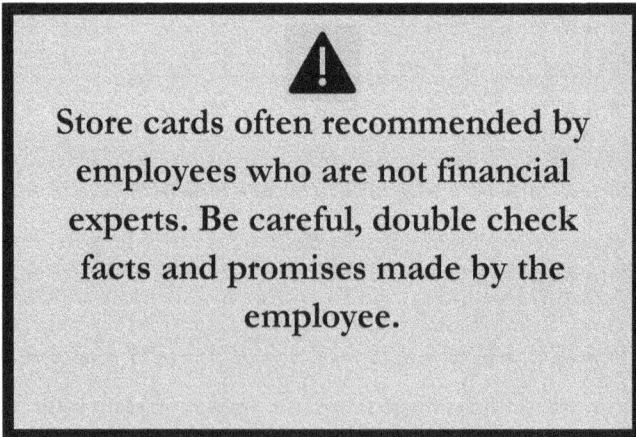

> ⚠️
>
> **Store cards often recommended by employees who are not financial experts. Be careful, double check facts and promises made by the employee.**

A third option: piggy-back on someone else's account.

This is a great solution for anyone who is lucky enough to have someone in their life that is willing to take on the risk and responsibility of your debt. This type of arrangement gives you all the advantages that established card holders get. Lower interest opportunities. rate, higher limits, no fees, etc.

The above options are great tools for you to utilize to begin growing and improving your credit. If these strategies are implemented wisely you will be well on your way to becoming more attractive to banks and be a great candidate for more and better free money opportunities.

You should be aware that each new credit application hurts your score for around 5 points if you have bad or limited credit. So, because of this it is smart to use the above-mentioned techniques to build up your score before you start filling out applications that are going to require an inquiry.

I talk more about timing and other factors that affect your score in the next section. But before that I feel I should say that there have been times when I was a little over zealous in my efforts and "counted my chickens before they hatch". There were a few deals that I worked on that, in the beginning, seemed to offer amazing return. I patted myself on the back for being so smart. But, after the dust settled and the actual results from the contract came to light my expectations were not met. I have learned that sometimes the words written in an agreement can be a little ambiguous and it was my job to make sense out of what I was reading. My bad!

Reading and understanding fine print is another topic we will cover later down the line.

Six: Building Your Credit Card Portfolio

(For those with Good or Better Numbers)

Great, you're one of the lucky ones that's ready to dig in and really get moving! Since you already have a good start because of your good numbers creditors love you. You are in the perfect position to start shopping around for the best deals in credit cards.

The first thing you would want to do is take an inventory of what accounts you already have in your library and what those accounts offer. Once you know exactly where you stand you should take a timeout and examine your needs. Decide what is missing in your library.

Ask yourself some questions:

- Where do I most commonly spend my money?

- What are my immediate goals?

- What are my long-term goals?

> ## The key is not to prioritize what's on your schedule, but to schedule your priorities.
> - Stephen Covey
>
> WWW.VERYBESTQUOTES.COM

Once you have identified your personal list of wants and needs you can match the right types of credit lines to address the objectives you have identified and given priority status.

This is a good time to bring up an important skill we all must master to really be successful with these strategies.

For those of us who live within a budget, (and really, who doesn't?) it is important to acquire the necessary skills that enable us to evaluate our desires critically and objectively. In doing so we can determine want from need and adjust our priorities accordingly.

We will go farther into the process of looking at wants verses needs in the following section.

For now, let's address the holes you have discovered in your library. Now you will begin hunting for the best options to fill those holes. This step sets you up and prepares you to plan your personal attack strategy!

First thing to do is to get ready to spend some time communicating with the banks in which you already have cards. Make a list of all your accounts and the websites and phone numbers so you can either contact them directly or go to their websites to see who's offering what. Be on the lookout for the best types of rewards for your lifestyle and goals.

Not everyone will want the same type of spiff. For instance, people who travel a lot will might be interested in travel points to use towards air fare, rental cars, hotel accommodations or whatever. For other people, a basic cash back point system could be the best option. If you are extra industrious you might even want to try juggling multiple cards at one time, each with differing types of rewards. By doing this you can really maximize the power of cash back rewards. Take advantage of rotating monthly or quarterly rewards. There are cards out there that give you as much as five percent back on purchases at or for pre-determined categories and retailers. To see the greatest results, you could use one card at gas stations, a different one for groceries, and yet another one for dining out and so on. I actually do this myself. Keep in mind that this strategy does require quite a bit of organization. I will go into record keeping and organization later. Suffice it to say that juggling these cards is a little tricky but well worth the effort.

Knowing what you already have on-hand will clearly demonstrate what you are lacking. It is simple to find the cards that offer the kind of rewards you need with a simple Google search. Personally, I like and subscribe to moneytalksnews.com for awesome tips on all things financial.

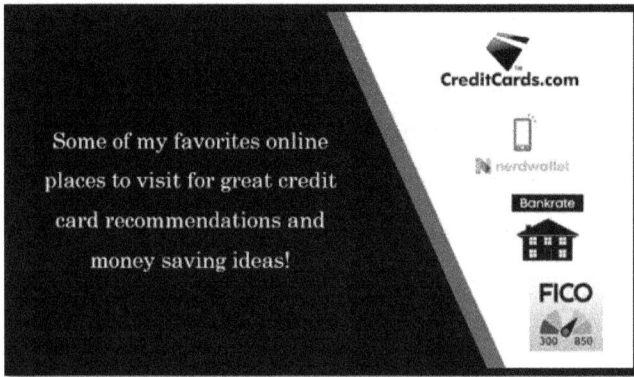

Some of my favorites online places to visit for great credit card recommendations and money saving ideas!

CreditCards.com

nerdwallet

Bankrate

FICO
300   850

You should be able to find a card to fill every need. With the right numbers, you will have no problem qualifying for the cards. Another plus is that every time you are rewarded with a new account your available credit to usage ratio get smaller, which in turn, improves your scores. We will talk about setting priorities and short-term goals a little later in the program. Once you have made these decisions you have created a path that will become your navigational tool. This tool will dictate exactly what type of rewards you will be looking for. Then just do your searches and take some notes. This is a good time to determine a timeline. I recommend that once you have decided which accounts will meet your present goals that you keep a list and set up a timeline for applications. I'll give you some tips for coming up with a great record keeping later. FICO says that people who have six or more inquiries on their credit reports are eight times more likely to default than those with less. It takes a couple of years for an inquiry to drop from your report. For this reason, you do not want to do too many applications at one time.

Now there are exceptions to this rule. People with excellent credit (a FICO score of 800 and up) often have success just waiting 3 months between applications. A rule of thumb, a six-month waiting period between applications is a good baseline for most people to follow.

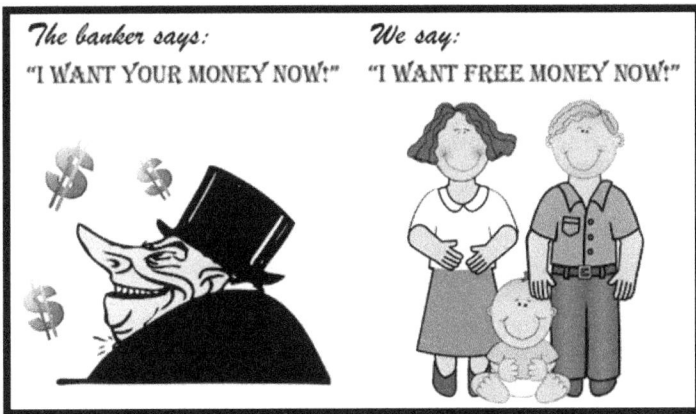

The banker says: "I WANT YOUR MONEY NOW!" We say: "I WANT FREE MONEY NOW!"

If you're not getting approved take another look at your reports and consider these statistics.

- 35% of your score comes from your payment history. If this is a problem for you. Fix this habit now! Time is the only remedy for a late payer's score.

- 30% of your score is determined by your how much total debt you have. Keep your usage ratio at or below 30% of your available on each account and all accounts combined. If this is your problem, review the steps and techniques we discussed previously and put them to work.

- 15% of your credit score comes from the length of your credit history. This is another reason it is important to keep your oldest accounts open. Accounts with a zero or very small balance also add to your total available credit which helps keep your ratio looking good.

- 10% of your score is determined by how much new credit you report. Of course, the only thing that helps this and the length of your history is the passage of time. Be patient. It's worth the wait!

- And finally, the last 10% is based on the types of cards in your portfolio. Store cards, prepaid cards, or major cards. This is such a small factor that I wouldn't worry too much about it.

If you don't that any of factors are an issue it's a good idea to call the credit card company that turned you down and get specific reasons for their decision. This information will help you on your next attempt. The point is this: the time to wait between credit card applications depends on several of your personal financial factors. Use the above information to help you make informed decisions about application process, and you'll be on your way to creating a good credit portfolio and raising your credit score.

Use debt consolidation to boost your scores even higher.

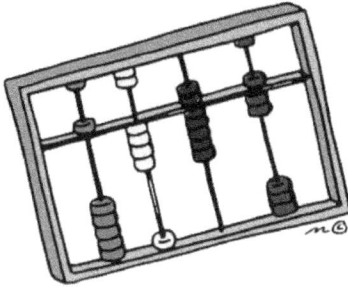

Debt consolidation is a form of debt management that allows you to find a way out from under debt while keeping your good standing. Debt consolidation allows for you to use one loan to a pay off all other accounts and loans you have leaving you with one monthly payment and interest rate. The way this helps your credit score is that it pays off your current accounts and leaves you with only one outstanding balance. Also, when you open another loan account you lower your credit availability to usage ratio.

There are many debt consolidation companies and with any consumer driven industry there are fly-by-night scam companies to watch out for. When looking for a debt consolidation company take the time to do a little research and learn as much as the company as you can. If Possible, ask for references and learn from other people who have experienced the company and staff members. The company and its employees should be trained and certified to work on debt consolidation cases and offer debt consolidation loans that are of reputable quality.

Before contacting a debt consolidation company, you should take the time to get your debt in order. This includes making a list of all the debt you want to include in the debt consolidation. For each item on your list include the following things:

Creditor and creditor contact information monthly payment amounts interest rate and current balance amounts

This gives you a clear idea of the debt you have and basic information about each one.

This is often one of the hardest parts of debt consolidation. You have to look at the whole picture and if you haven't been keeping track along the way, it can be overwhelming.

Debt consolidation can also be followed by other debt management tactics, like debt negotiation, that can help to minimize the debt to allow you to take out a smaller loan and save you more money overall. Many credit counselors are trained in the art of debt negotiation and should offer that as a service with your debt consolidation. When you negotiate your current debt, you can settle at a lower amount than the current balance, which helps your debt consolidation loan and your repayment over the life of the loan.

If you are looking for a way to help your credit rating and score, debt consolidation could be the right choice for you. Debt consolidation is a smart way to get rid of debt while still preserving integrity on your credit report and can boost your credit rating. When all your debts are paid, this changes the status of the account and when your credit score is recalculated it should reflect this new positive status and boost your credit score. This can bring you hope and instant success in getting your debt under control.

Seven: Wants verses Needs

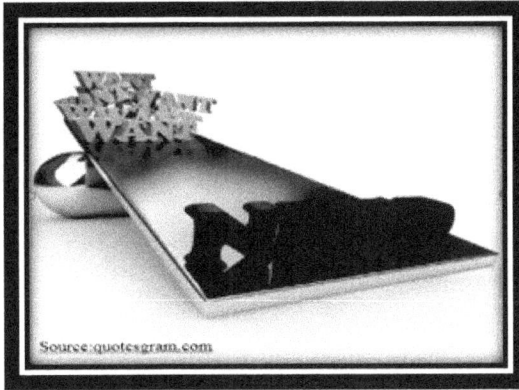

Source: quotesgram.com

In 1954 Abraham Maslow published *Motivation and Personality* where his theory, "Maslow's Hierarchy of Needs", was explained.

In a nutshell, the theory states that human beings grow as they attain one level of need and then they move on to move to the next higher level. He suggests that the most basic level of needs must be met before people will have a strong motivation to move onto the next, higher level. The need for food, shelter, and clothing must be met before we will even want greater things. I believe that most people would agree with the notion that there is an innate hierarchy of needs in the human experience, but even with that being true we will certainly find that some needs are situational.

In today's world, there are expectations placed upon us that require more stuff than the basic needs expressed in Maslow's hierarchy. There will be times when our situation will dictate additional needs. At first glance, these things could mistakenly be viewed as wants but because we cannot avoid them they should now be under the category of need. There will be dress codes to adhere to, places we cannot reasonable get to without our own transportation, professional expectations that must be met, and so on.

The point is this. Don't get too hung up on labels when evaluating wants verses needs. Don't fail to recognize that there will be times that new needs will pop up and be worthy of a closer look so that you can determine what category they really fit. Just go with it and make allowances for the unavoidable. Don't fight it when something you may have always considered a want presents itself as a *need*.

SET PRIORITIES

An excellent and easy way to decide on priorities is Stephen R. Covey's Time Management Quadrant. You'll want to get a big piece of paper and draw out the quadrant, but leave the shapes empty of text.

Now consider what the quadrants are all about.

- Things listed in section I are both urgent and important. These are often things that have a deadline or are in other ways time specific. It will include thing that need to be done now or you have a disaster on your hands.

- Things listed in section II are important, but not urgent. It's your personal goals, the things you want to realize in your life.

- Things listed in section III and IV are things that you can let go of, or at least put on the back burner while you are doing the things in the first two sections.

I'll give you an example. Let's say you just received an invitation for your tenth-year high school graduation reunion. You assess that it should be listed in section II. You really want to attend (it is important to you), but it is not going to create disaster if you don't go. You have only one obstacle to overcome; you really feel like you shouldn't spend the money. After all, the plane ticket, hotel room and dazzling new outfits are going to cost some bucks!

Even with all that weighing on your mind you decide to go for it. You have a few months to come up with a killer plan to do this in the most beneficial way possible.

This is a perfect time to put your new skills to work!

You've done the math and figure the whole trip including all the goodies is going to run you about $1500. You think you can comfortable pay for about half of the trip with cash. Great start. Now you only need to come up with the other $750.

You understand that you will be using some cash, but is that really the case? Not necessarily.

Let's talk about that. Even your "cash" can be a credit card if you pay it off when the bill comes in. In fact, in my opinion this is the best way to do things. Remember, you are using a reward generating card. Every time you use that card instead of actual cash you get a cash return.

The very first thing I always do is jump on-line and start looking at discount gift cards. A few websites for discount gift cards are:

- Gift Card Granny

- Raise

- Card Pool

- Gift Card Zen

On good days I find gift cards to my favorite stores and restaurants for as much as 56% off their face value! You will also find gift cards for hotels and motels at fabulous discounts. If you purchase the gift cards with your best cash back rewards card, you have upped you discount by at least another 1.5%. If you have opened a new account that will give you an extra $100-$300 for spending X amount of dollars in the first 90 days, you can add that right to the top of your budget. Take these discounts into mind and then see how much farther your cash will go.

By shopping with discount gift cards, you have already begun winning the game. You have stacked savings upon savings!

Let's look at some real numbers.

Okay. Let's say you could snag some gift cards to a place you love to shop. The cards' face values add up to $300, you only paid $225 for the cards with the 25% discount. You put the discounted gift cards on your best cash back credit card. Let's say they are offering 3% cash back rewards any purchase. That's another $6.75 that you can add to the initial $75.00. Now you'll have $81.75 off your $300-dollar purchase. You have paid $218.25 for a $300 purchase!

Eight: Find the Best Deals

There are many ways for you to find great deals and freebies when you make it a habit to do these easy things before you go on your regular shopping adventures! These practices will soon become a way of life and you will never forget to do them.

In fact, I get a rush every time I find a way to win! This is where my motto of beating them at their own game came from. Now, I have to really work at convincing myself to purchase things that I have *not* found a way to save on.

If I know that I will visiting a particular restaurant on a regular basis (and sometimes even it's just one time!) I make sure to join their frequent shoppers club. Most of the restaurants that have these clubs send out weekly or monthly emails with unadvertised sales, coupons, and special promotions. I know I always get a coupon for a free dessert from Olive Garden to use in the month of my birthday. Some restaurants offer free appetizers or buy one get one free meal offers for your birthday. I get several of these offers every June. What a nice treat! Once a year I grab a

friend and head out to the
Olive Garden for a free
piece of Tiramisu and a cup
of coffee. Beef O Brady's
sends me savings coupons
that I use or pass onto one
of my friends when we meet
for our monthly lunch. In
fact, I have plans to meet some friends for lunch next week at a place I
have never been to before, so I went to their website today and signed up
for their club. They sent me a coupon for a free appetizer. Who says
there's no such thing as a free lunch?!

These are not the only ways I save when I eat out I also go online before
an engagement and check their website and coupon sites for any deals
that may be offered that I might have missed.

Do you scour the Sunday paper sales inserts?

Make it a habit to look for special offers before hitting the stores.
Whether you are shopping for a new shirt or a big-ticket item there are
several things you can do to make smart buying decisions.

Do you know how to negotiate?

Many people find the idea of negotiating for a better deal a little
intimidating. I personally like the act of haggling. This is all part of the
game. The better you are at it the more you win. I'm sure that when you
take the time to listen to and learn from the best negotiators doing it for
yourself will be much easier.

We will look at how to be an effective negotiator after this next section, But, first let's look at some shopping tips and strategies to help you find the best deals and save you some big money!

I.   Shop with a list.

This just seems like common sense, but it really works. It is much easier to resist temptation that might lead to an impulse buy. A list keeps you accountable to yourself. Sometimes it's good to give yourself a little extra push to make the right decision.

II.   Know the shopping seasons.

You can save BIG on seasonal and holiday merchandise if you wait until the end of the season to shop. There are other ways to save. Recognize that stores put certain merchandise categories on sale in certain months. Computers, school and office supplies in the fall back to school sales. Since home improvement projects often are put on hold during the summer because of family vacations, look for home repair merchandise sales in June and July.

III.   Use rewards cards for your purchases.

The first thing I always do is make sure that I have my best cash back rewards card with me. I have been talking about using these cards to compound your best deals on everything you buy forever. I am not suggesting that you should pile up debt, but rather you use your cards to make the initial purchase and then pay your balance in full by the at the end of the month. If you allow debt to accumulate you will defeating the whole purpose. You are using the cards to get something for nothing. Your reward. Interest will surely put a dent in or eat up any advantage you have gained with the cash back rewards.

IV. Search for unadvertised deals.

There are lots of places online where bargain hunters can go to get coupons and find unadvertised and flash deals. When you check these sites regularly you get the down low on specials that many people don't ever even see. You will find rebate offers, online-only coupons and last-minute deals that retailors often run for overstock items, one-of-a-kinds, scratch and dent, etc. You will also find reviews for products and the deal itself.

V. Look for goods and services at discount sites.

Local service providers and smaller, privately owned businesses use sites like Groupon and LivingSocial to find new customers by offering their goods and services at a discount. I have gotten some very steep discounts on services

VI. Earn money from cash back shopping sites.

Use sites like Ebates.com, Upromise, and Extrabux for opportunities for cash back when you shop online. Your purchases are seen bey the cash back site and you reap cash back goodies!

VII. Use shopping apps.

Some of these apps use crowdsourcing to get you in-the-know and some of them let you scan the barcode then the app does the comparing for you. Here's a list of a few excellent shopping apps. You'll love them for locating discounts and comparison shopping include:

- **Slickdeals**: You'll learn about discounts and then be able to follow a link to the online retailer offer the deal. You can also shop by your location.

- **PriceBlink**: This is a browser add-on. You will be alerted when sopping online if a lower price is found elsewhere. According to the maker, users save an average of 17% to 20% on every purchase!

- **Favado:** Does the legwork for you. It surveys 65,000 grocery and drugstores. You use the app to you can decide where to shop and then build your list accordingly.

- **Coupons.com**: You will find thousands of coupons on everyday products. Go here before you hit the stores!

- **RedLaser:** This barcode scanning app lets you compare prices on items right in the store and when purchasing from your phone.

- **PriceGrabber:** Like RedLaser, this app lets you scan products for a better deal elsewhere and it alerts you when the item you went meets the price you have specified.

- **RetailMeNot:** Collects codes form coupons and other sale information from retailers. You can bookmark your favorite stores to check later when shopping for the best deal.

VIII. **Sleep on the idea of making major purchases and splurges.**

I do this for almost everything I can testify that I have saved myself thousands of dollars when the new day comes, and I have decided I shouldn't get the item for one reason or another. If you decide after a couple of days that this is still something you want, go for it!

IX. **Let you're a service HUH? XX do some comparative shopping** *after* **you buy.**

For example, there is the Citi Price Rewind service available to eligible Citi cardholders. You simply register your qualifying purchase and Citi Price Reward searches hundreds of retailor sites and if the same item is found for $25 less and within 30 days for your purchase Citi Price Rewind will refund you the difference. All the way up to $250!

X.   Add up all the charges.

This is another tip that seems like a no-brainer and plain old common sense, but I will still bring it up. Make sure you know exactly what the shipping and handling charges are, if any. These added fees must be making money for the sellers, or they wouldn't have them.

XI.   Fill in the promo box.

You can quickly leap away from your purchase and look for promotions, coupons and other discounts that the retailer might be offering. Check out any credit card reward that you might be able to apply. Do a search on other sites, like FreeShopping.org. Why pay full price when you can save by investing a few minutes?

By waiting to buy things, by doing my homework, and by visiting sites like the Better Business Bureau before I commit to a purchase I am confident that I am making the right decision.

> **Win or lose, we go shopping after the election**
> **-- Imelda Marcos**

Now, let's move on to negotiation skills.

It would be a great thing if learning the power of influence was something taught in public school. It's something that would behoove anyone. Having the ability to effectively negotiate creates a powerful presence that other's respond to with respect and reverence. The power to negotiate will help you get that raise, get a better deal on a car and just be a more convincing speaker in general.

Here are some specific points on negotiation techniques:

I.   You can negotiate just about everything.

Don't believe that the price tag is always the final word. Just like we negotiate for big ticket items we can also do it for every day purchases and even our utilities. Ask the sale clerk if there are any incentives to be had. Always talk to your providers like credit cards, internet and the electric company for any perks they offer. If you are not happy many times you can negotiate a better deal. They would rather give you a better deal than lose your business.

II.   Be prepared.

If you enter a negotiation unprepared you are halfway to losing already. Know exactly what you want and be prepared to say it. This is no time to hide your assertive side. Do some research so you know what your opponent must get from the deal as to not make unreasonable demands.

III.   Listen with both ears.

Learning how to listen quietly is a great characteristic for anyone who wants to master the art of negotiation. Let the other person state their side. Encourage them to talk first There's an old negotiation maxim that says: whoever mentions numbers first, loses. If they don't bring up numbers, you have the chance to ask them what they are thinking.

IV.   If you don't ask for it, you won't get it.

Before the negotiation starts you should have already determined what your bottom line is, or maybe I should say your top line. That is, what is your highest justifiable price? If you can deliver a convincing argument aim high and go for your best price. Stay away from ultimatums like "Take it or leave it" leave that to the sharks on Shark Tank!

V.   Be ready to compromise.

You should be ready and expect to concessions. Think ahead of time as to what they might be. It is a good practice to never take the first offer. If they give an offer that is better than you expected there is no reason you can't try to look or sound disappointed to see if you can get an even better offer!

VI.   Their problems are their problems!

You will most likely hear all the reasons they can't meet you offer because of this issue or that problem. That is on them, not you! Stick to your guns, offer a solution if you can. For instance, if you are asking for a better price on piece of electronics and they are telling you no, offer to get a matching accessory or some extra stuff that you will need anyway.

Beware! Small print alert!

We live in a time of terms and conditions and we have never before signed or agreed so many. But one thing hasn't changed: we still rarely read them.

According to a Fairer Finance survey, for some companies now runs to more than 30,000 words (the length of a short novel) and, unsurprisingly, 73% of people admit to not reading all the fine print. Of those who do, only 17% say they understand it (Glancy).

With these statistics in mind I will attempt to take some of the mystery out of small print.

Let's look at a Credit Card Jargon Buster!

Credit cards, as part of the financial industry, use a massive array of jargon. You can't be expected to recognize all these technical terms, and some of them are quite important – so here's a quick guide, in alphabetical order.

- **Affinity card**

  This is a credit card that gives a certain amount to a charity of your choice, depending on how much you spend. It is generally best to avoid any charity that wants you to sign up for such a card – don't let guilt lead you to a high interest rate.

- **APR**

  Annual Percentage Rate. This is your overall interest rate, calculated yearly, and given as a percentage of your balance.

- **ATM**

  Automated Teller Machine. I'm sure everyone is aware of this term, but I thought I would include it remind everyone that many times you will be charged for using an ATM that is outside the cards issuers group.

- **Balance transfer**

  This is when you transfer your debt("balance") from one credit card to another. The usual reason people do this (and the reason I do!) to keep debt on lower-interest cards.

- **Compound interest**

  The addition of interest to the principal sum of a loan. In other words, interest on interest! It is the result of reinvesting interest, rather than paying it out, so that interest in the next period is then earned on the principal sum plus previously-accumulated interest. A very bad thing!

- **Credit limit**

  Your credit limit is the maximum amount you can spend or withdraw from your card. Going over your credit limit will most certainly result in your card not being accepted when trying to make a purchase (how embarrassing!), and the bank will charge you for this embarrassment with an over limit fee. OUCH!

- **Fixed rate**

  A fixed rate card is one where you are given a rate when you sign up for the card and that rate, at least in theory, stays the same for the whole time you have the card. In the real world though, interest rates can change for almost any reason.

- **Grace period**

  Your grace period is the amount of time between when you spend money and when you start paying interest on it. Good cards can have a grace period of up to two months – bad ones might not have one at all. Most are to the next billing cut-off date.

- **Minimum payment**

  A minimum payment is the absolute lowest amount you can pay back to the credit card company each month – you should always pay more, this is so important I will say it again. You should always pay more! I know you don't have to but doing so looks very good on you. Minimum payments are usually around 2% of your balance.

- **Sub-prime**

  This is a phrase used in the industry to describe customers who are a bad credit risk, but are still seen as worthy for loans anyway. If you are identified as sub-prime, you'll start getting offers for loans secured on your property. They know that if you can't pay, they'll get their money anyway. So, obviously agreeing to this is not something to take lightly.

- **Teaser rate**

> I have always said that everyone is in sales. Maybe you don't hold the title of salesperson, but if the business you are in requires you to deal with people, you, my friend, are in sales.
>
> -Zig Ziglar

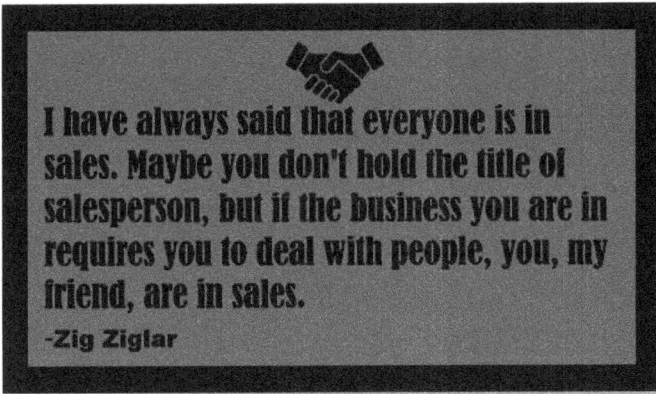

A 'special offer' low rate, usually written in enormous letters. You will see many offers with "LOW 4.9% APR" in inch-high letters, followed by "for first six months, 21.9% thereafter" in microscopic ones. Teaser offers can sometimes be worth taking, but not if they tie you in for longer than the period of the offer. I do this a lot, but I keep excellent records. You must have a great record keeping system in place if these offers are going to really work well for you. We look at record keeping in the next chapter.

- **Variable rate**

  This is an interest rate that is worked out by adding a certain amount to the current base rate. Taking this option will allow your credit card to be affected by changes in national interest rates – a good idea if you think they might go down, and a bad one if they're on the way up. You will find that most cards are set up with variable rates.

Avoid Payment Holidays.

After paying on a credit card a while, you might be offered a "payment holiday". You get a letter saying that since the company knows it's difficult for some families around Christmas (or whatever other excuse they think up), they're offering you a month off from paying, as a "special present".

Why do they do this? Well, for them to make more money of course!

These offers typically have a high acceptance rate. People think it's great that they can take a month off from paying back debt. What they don't understand is that these "holidays" aren't a present at all! They're a hidden money generator for the credit card company. For the company, it's a win: they get to make big profits just by making their most stressed customers happy. It's definitely dirty pool!

If you read the small print, you'll find that the payment holiday isn't interest free! You're still being charged interest and since you're not paying anything back that month, the interest will be there next month for you to pay more interest on (compound interest, you see).

<u>An example to clarify</u>. Let's say you were paying back $1,000 of debt at 1.5% per month (about 19.5% per year). Your minimum payment each month is 2% (26.82% per year).

If you pay the minimum for all 12 months of the year, then you will pay back $233.51, and owe $941.62 at the end of the year. Your debt has been reduced by $58.38, and you've lost $175.13 in interest.

With the payment holiday, though, you pay 2% per month for only 11 months (so you pay 24.3% back on the debt over the year). That's $217.80, and you'd owe $960.55 at the end of the year. Overall, you've paid $37.86 for your payment holiday from a payment of about $20. In other words, your month off will cost you almost two months of payments.

Don't worry if you don't understand all the math involved here – it's been deliberately designed by mathematicians and marketers to be as confusing as possible, so you don't see the bigger picture and catch on to how bad a deal this really is.

Just remember: don't fall for it. The more you owe, the more that "holiday" will cost you. Wouldn't you rather take your money and go on a real holiday, instead of spending it all on repaying credit card debt? This is like everything else in life. No one gives you anything for nothing – least of all credit card companies. Anytime they offer you anything, it's because they're going to make a profit on it, or at least that's their plan! But your reading this and you are learning how to take advantage of their greed and turn it around on them.

Credit Card Checks and Cash Advances.

Once you've got a credit card, you'll find that you can do more with it than just pay for things with the card. You might be sent credit card checks to use when you're paying someone who doesn't accept cards, or when you want a cash advance.

Cash advance: a way to withdrawal cash directly from your credit card, either to your bank account or from a cash machine. This is designed for when you need cash in an emergency. You really shouldn't overuse either of these features because you could pay more interest.

Sometimes checks and advances are charged at a much higher rate of interest than normal spending. You often give up any interest-free period (as much as two months), meaning that you start paying interest on the money literally from the minute you receive it. Not only that, many times there a fee associated with checks and cash advances. The fees are usually 3% to 5% of the transaction. That is in addition to the much higher interest rate you find with these offers. Using an ATM may increase the fee even further.

The following was taken from a 2015 article on creditcards.com

"Consumers who take cash advances with a credit card will pay for that quick, convenient service, regardless of whether they have good credit and a low purchase APR.

Only 13 cards base individual cardholder's cash advance APRs on creditworthiness and none offer cardholders an APR lower than the corresponding purchase APR. Most cards -- 86 out of 100 -- charge a cash advance APR higher than 20 percent.

Among the cards surveyed, those with the highest cash advance APRs are:

- First Premier Bank credit card: 36 percent

- BP Visa and Texaco Visa: 29.99 percent

- ExxonMobil SmartCard: 29.95 percent

- Shell Platinum MasterCard: 27.99 percent

Cost of a $1,000 cash advance

Even if you pay it off quickly, cash advances are costly compared to credit card purchases. For example, if you purchase a $1,000 item on a credit card with a 14.99 percent rate -- today's national average for new cards -- and pay it off in 30 days, you'll pay $1,000. You escape paying interest, thanks to the grace period. But a $1,000 cash advance under the typical terms our survey found will cost you $69.34. That includes the $50 upfront fee, and $19.34 for 30 days' interest at 23.53 percent (Kossman).

These numbers are frightening for sure! But I still employ these types of offers all the time and get a great deal with them. This just highlights once again how vitally important it is to keep accurate records and stay on top of what's happening with your accounts.

When you receive an offer that allows you to move or borrow a large balance to a card that has a minimal transaction fee. Let's say 1 to 3%, and they give you 18 or more months of interest free financing it's a great thing! But, if you forget and don't keep up with when the offer expires and allow the balance to start acquiring all that interest you have **not** won the game!

It is good to use the card for daily purchases instead.

Instead of using cash to pay for small things and finding you have to take advances or use checks to pay for bigger things, it's better to do it the other way around. If you're in a situation where you're relying on advances, you should start using your card for smaller things where you wouldn't usually bother, just to avoid taking the advances and paying more interest. Be strategic in how you spend.

Look Out for Advance Limits.

Eventually you could run into an advance limit. Many credit cards have limits on how much of your balance can be cash advances and how much must be in purchases. Find out these limits before you start taking advances.

Understanding the Terms and Conditions.

When you're looking at a credit card offers take a good, long look at the small print; it's vitally important. If you're lucky there will an easy to read "summary box" that outlines the terms of the credit card agreement. These always make understanding the agreement a breeze.

I hate to say this, but credit card lenders can be devious, and there are plenty of things there designed to slip you up. Here's some things for you to be on your guard against.

- **Annual Fees**

  Even though you're already paying them interest, many credit cards still charge you an annual fee. It's not as common as it once was, but it's still around. You should be especially careful to check for fees on Gold and Platinum cards – even though they're not that hard to get any more, they still tend to charge much higher fees than normal cards. And, who card what color the card is. Ridiculous

- **Penalty Charges**

  Pay attention to what kind of fees you'll be charged for a late payment, or if you take a cash advance, or if you accidentally exceed your limit on the card. Some cards have unjustifiably high fees. Don't sign up for them.

- **Interest Method**

  This is one of the most overlooked of all the things in the small print, just because it's so hard to understand. Essentially, every company has a slightly different way of working out how much interest you should pay each month. There are three main methods:

- **The adjusted balance method.**

  You are charged interest on whatever your balance was when the company sent the bill. Another version of this is,

- **The previous balance.**

  You're charged interest on your balance as it stood at the end of the billing cycle before this one, regardless of how much you've spent or paid off since. Odd, but easier to understand.

- **The average daily balance.**

  This is the most complicated, but also the most common now. Your balance from the end of each day in the billing cycle is added up, and then divided by how many days there were, and interest is charged on this amount. This method is only good for you if your balance jumps around a lot, as it avoids you paying lots of interest on a balance that just happened to be large on the billing date.

  Also, make sure you look at the rate of interest each month, instead of just relying on the APR. The APR is an estimate of the total cost of borrowing – it is the monthly interest plus the various charges that will show you exactly how much you would pay.

- **Grace Period.**

  Check that the card you're looking at has a grace period on

purchases. Otherwise, you could end up being charged interest from the minute you spend.

- **Currency Conversion Fees.**

  If you plan to use your card abroad, you should take a look at how much the card charges for transactions made in other currencies. Some cards can be much more expensive than others.

  When you pay back your credit card debt, some lenders will put your payments towards the lowest-interest money (your purchases) first, and then towards other lending. Just make sure you understand how and what they do and plan accordingly.

Nine: Dirty Trick Men!

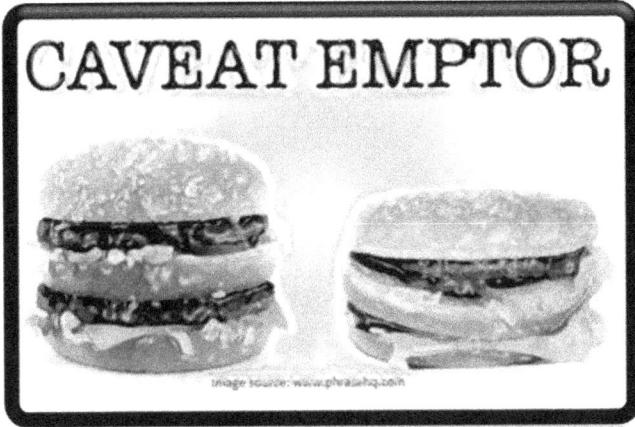

What is a dirty trick man?

These guys are everywhere, in every industry, and such a huge problem that I hardly know where to begin!

I guess I will introduce this section by bringing up what could arguable be the one of the most harmful dirty tricks that this country has ever suffered. This event changed how many people view our world and relate to the American dream. Many, many people are still reeling from and trying to recover from it.

I am referring to the housing bubble disaster of 2008 and the resulting economic meltdown.

I will not get into the details that surround this awful event, but I will go on record to say that if it were not for some greedy, dirty trick men this would have never happened, and countless people would still be living happily ever after in their beautiful new homes.

This is a perfect, although extreme example, of the damage that can be done when people are out of control, and only concerned with making an easy buck.

Inflation-adjusted U.S home prices, Population, Building Costs, and Bond Yields (1890-2005)

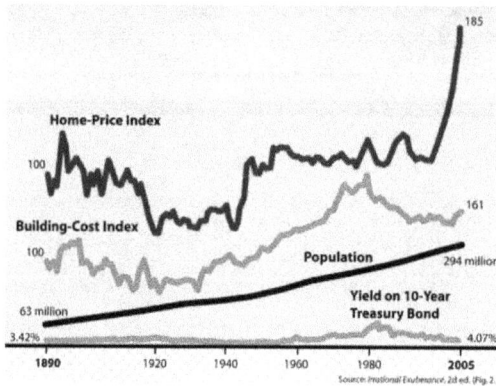

Source: *Irrational Exuberance*, 2d ed. (Fig. 2.1)

Section 1 - Retail tricks

It happens all the time. The typical story goes something like this: On your way home from a hard day at work you stop at the local Walmart Family market to pick up a loaf of bread for the kids lunches tomorrow and some Blue Bell ice cream for a yummy late-night snack. No matter what, it seems like we always end up with a lot more things in our shopping cart than what we had planned and a lot less left in our wallet than we had anticipated.

You find yourself lugging 2 or 3 bags full of stuff back to the car and realize that you have bought 3 times what you had originally planned and spent that much more out of your carefully planned budget as well. Blowing your budget every time you step foot in a store can have devastating effects on your life and your health. The stress that comes with money problems literally kill marriages, people, and dreams!

How do they do it and why do we always seem to fall for it?

Well, there's an easy answer to that question. The blame can be placed squarely placed on the shoulder of marketers and the magic they do. There are entire industries built on finding ways to separate us from our money. And these people are good at what they do!

Let's, for a minute look at some of the tactics that retailors commonly use to trick us into over purchasing and over spending.

The BOGO (buy on get one free)

My favorite grocery store is Publix. They consistently rank as the number one grocery chain in the south-east. There's good reason for that in that have the best customer service anyone will find anywhere. Publix constantly runs BOGO's in their weekly ad. Now, at first glance this looks like a great deal. Sometimes it really is, but rarely all on its own. I have found that almost without exception BOGOs are run on items that have an inflated regular price.

Make sure that the deal is really a deal before you buy. Check on-line for competitor prices and make the critical decision of do I really need 2 of this item before you buy. If the item is perishable be sure you will use it before it is too late. They don't care that you are buying twice you need and end up throwing it out. In fact, they love it.

There is one way to use these types of sales really make them pay off. Of course, this will require a little leg-work. Coupons. I know, I know, you're thinking really, you have got to be kidding me!

No, I am not kidding! At most stores, they will allow people to stack manufacturers coupons on top of store coupons on top of the BOGOs. Many time I have gotten things for free using this strategy.

This has been a successful strategy for me at CVS. The ExtraCare program is wonderful. With a little planning, I have saved huge. I always do some homework before I make my monthly trip to the drugstore. I check out the ad online, get my coupons, digital and paper, together, and then I take advantage of their ExtraCare program. Cha ching!

What we offer is better than what you already have.

How many times have you ended up on a shopping channel when channel surfing and found that the item they were show-casing was just so tempting?

Of course, that is no accident. The sets they use on these shopping channels are designed specifically with getting the viewer to phone in and buy. Oh my gosh, that huge pillow-top bed looks so nice! You almost need a ladder to get to get in it; those sheets and comforter sure look sumptuous with the matching curtains, rugs, and pillows! I want it! Okay, now back to reality. They are using emotion to get into your head. They have hired experts in consumer behavior, and merchanded their displays to appeal to you and boost their sales. Beware!

Psst, look over here

The use of "Neuromarketing" teaches retail managers how to display and advertise their wares. Unlike TV they get to appeal to all your senses to get you to buy! Why do you think the bakery and produce is in the front of the store? They know that when you walk in and smell the fresh-baked bread your mouth will be watering and begging you to take it home. That stack of luscious fresh fruit is begging you, "buy me".

Oh boy, look at the flashy signs and good stuff at the end of every isle. They make sure that you don't miss seeing the fanciest labeled, most exotic brands of olive oil by placing them right at eye level. Can't you just imagine yourself standing in front of your stove using that delicious olive oil to sauté some of the fresh veggies you just placed in your cart?

You better make sure you really want and need that little, $10 bottle of olive oil before you put it in your cart! After all, doesn't the brand with the plain label that is just a third its price still sauté those veggies?

Don't you need this too?

How many times, after agonizing on what pair of shoes to get, do you reach the checkout just to have the cashier show you something you must purchase to go with your new shoes? If you didn't need it when you picked out your shoes, you probably don't need it now!

The loss leader

By giving items such a low sale price the store is losing money on the item. They lure you into the store in the hopes that they can then sell you other items to go along with the deal. For instance, I see this a lot with fresh strawberries. You run to the store to take advantage of the wonderful price on those strawberries and see the shortcakes and whipped cream displayed right there with them. You think to yourself, hum. I need those things too. So, you go for it. Gotcha!

Smaller packages

Have you noticed the little min-cans of soda that are in the supermarkets now? Research has shown that contrary to what they claim the intent is in packaging things in smaller containers people end up consuming more that if they had bought in bulk. They (the food industry) have tried to convince us that this is their way of trying to help to eliminate the problem of weight gain. Yea right, my left foot!

What they have accomplished is getting people to pay more for less, and at the same time, waste natural resources. Shame on them!

Where are the artichoke hearts?

The stores have purposely made it hard to find some things by laying the merchandise out counter intuitively They know that if we get lost and wonder about the store we are more likely to buy impulsively. Also, the distraction that is created when we are thrown off our game when we get lost makes us less price sensitive, and therefore, less on guard to watch out for our wallets!

Rude, pushy salespeople

In one study, it was found that people are more inclined to buy more expensive products when the salesperson acts snotty to them. This tactic is employed by high-end stores like Gucci and other luxury brands. What? That's crazy? They get people to spend more by treating them bad!

The essential point is, know what you want before you go to the store. Be prepared with your savings weapons and stick to your list. Don't be seduced by pretty labels, fancy displays, and your own emotions.

Don't do it! Be smarter than the Dirty Trick men!

Section 2 - Credit Provider Tricks:

As you are aware there is always plenty of small print on the back page of the paperwork that comes with any new credit card. In that small print, they might be some of what I call 'credit card nasties' that can make your seemingly great new card actually be a real stinker.

Here are some of the fine print nasties you should be on the lookout for:

Tricky interest calculations

Calculating interest is often tricky and can be misleading. Credit card issuers like it that way. Don't let them fool you. Understand what type of interest you have signed up for and how to calculate it. There websites you can go to and it will do your calculations for you. I think that doing this is never a bad idea. You will know exactly how much to pay for how long to pay off a debt. Also, understand the terminology used in any agreement. You might need to break open a dictionary or read an article online, but that is a small price to pay to have the confidence to know that *you* are in control and know exactly what to expect. Smart!

> ## Just because you're paranoid does not mean they're not out to get you!

Minimum payments

Avoid making the minimum payment anytime you are using an account that is acquiring interest. If you are using an interest free card, of course it is okay to just make the minimum.

But if you're not you are looking at a trap! You could be setting yourself up for terrible financial trouble down the road.

Creditors tend to set up the minimum payment at 2% or $25 whichever is greater. You will be looking at making payments for the longest possible time and be adding up tons of interest when you only pay the minimum amount. It could even hurt your credit score.

There is usually a "Minimum Payment Warning" at the bottom of your bill. It has a table that shows how long it will take you to pay off your balance and how much money, over and above your initial debt, you will end up forking over to the credit card company. You will significantly shorten the life of the loan when you make larger payments. Twice as much cuts your time in half.

Those bigger interest charges will rack up fast!

Rates that change with a missed or late payment

Some contracts include a clause that states that they can raise your rate if you were to miss a payment or go over your limit. You could be enjoying a fabulous introductory rate of as little as 0% and see that rate jump to a mind numbing 30%. Be extra vigilant. Don't make this mistake!

Allocation of payments

If you are carrying two different types of balances on one card, you need to make sure you understand how your payments will be applied to the debt.

For example, you could have a balance that stems from a balance transfer from another, higher rate, card. At the same time, you could be carrying a balance that came from your regular purchases. Your balance transfer has a 0% interest rate and the purchases have an interest rate of 13%. You

need to know how much of your payment is applied to the higher rate charges verses the lower rate balance transfer amount. Obviously, you would want the purchases to be credited before the balance transfer. Be careful and pay attention. Don't let them get over on you!

Due dates that change.

It would be so easy to mess up your payment history if your card does not have a steady, static monthly payment due date. Some cards have a due date that will fluctuate. If yours does and you have your payments set up to automatically pay on a specific date, this could slip by and ruin a good thing. You might not even be aware of what happened until the next month's bill. Then you see a nasty late fee, and in the worst-case scenario, a higher interest rate has been applied to your remaining balance.

Credit "Protection"

This is supposed to make your payments for you if you become disabled or lose your job. This is like any other type of insurance and you could find yourself in an uphill battle to even use the benefit. Insurance companies are always looking for ways to get out of paying up, and this is no different. Avoid signing up for these kinds of add-ons. It is unlikely that it would ever even pay for itself, much less benefit you in any way. On the other hand, they credit card company gets to charge you every month and add that to their profits. Payment protection charges are normally calculated by charging you so much per dollar and then they add that right to your balance. You end up paying interest on the charge and if you ever do use it, normally it would only make the minimum payment for you anyway. Bad deal!

Credit card theft insurance

Straight up – you don't need it. If your card is stolen you are only liable for $50 at the most. Many times, you would not be held liable for any charges. This is a complete waste!

Extra charges for purchases made abroad

This is something I have seen a lot. There usually is a 1% currency exchange rate and some banks add another 2% in fees for charges (and debit card purchases) made outside the US. This could really add up!

Lowering your credit limit

You could originally have a $5,000 limit on your card and suddenly find that your limit has been decreased. Some companies are re-evaluating the amount of credit they have issued to card holders and, in some cases, they are decreasing the amount of certain people's credit lines. This will affect your available credit which in turn can ruin your careful plan of using 30% or less of your credit line, or even worse, put you over your limit so then they can raise your interest rate All this negatively impacts you credit report. I personally find this trick is especially dirty!

The Big Print Givith, And The Fine Print Taketh Away

--Fulton j. Sheen

Buy Here, Pay Here lots

No credit – no problem is what they will tell you while cash registers are cha-chinging in their heads. If your credit is shaky you could easily fall into the trap of a subprime auto loan. Here are some freighting statistics:

- Some finance companies are charging as much as 29.66 percent interest on used car loans
- Lots sometimes pricing cars at around 60 percent (some to the tune of $11,000) more than their Kelly Blue Book value
- Some cars have such bad mechanical problems that are inoperable within a week or two of purchase.
- Repositions are taking place in a little as 2 days after a missed payment.

The lack of regulations in the subprime auto loan industry gives people little to no recourse when faced with such dilemmas. But there are a few things you can do try to protect yourself.

- Ask for the Carfax report before deciding on a car.
- Have a trusted mechanic.
- Check the cars market value before you sign examine the vehicle
- Do the math to understand exactly how much you will end up paying for the vehicle.

Some more ideas for fighting back!

Credit card companies are required to notify you, in writing, whenever there is a change to your terms of service. So, this means you cannot just toss out mail you get form them before reading it. Unfortunately, this means reading that densely-written little booklet they include in their mailings. They are packed full of confusing credit jargon. It is up to you to do your homework, so you can protect yourself and your credit form misunderstandings. The best way you can protect yourself from credit card "nasties" is to stay on top of your credit. Sadly, banks often do their best to keep customers in the dark. Keep track of your interest rates and balances so that when changes happen, you'll notice them right away.

If it looks like your credit card company is trying to pull a fast one on you call customer service and voice your protest. I have found that more times than not they are willing to negotiate with me if I am in good standing (current on my account). I just politely ask them to refund the fee or reverse the change in terms. It sure doesn't hurt to ask, and it works a lot of the time. Remember you catch more flies with sugar than vinegar. That is especially true when dealing with customer service anywhere. A lot of times I have been given a free pass on the first time a late payment has happened. Sometimes it's even helpful to threaten to transfer your balance to another card, because ultimately, they want your money.

Section 3 - Service Provider Tricks

There are always traps in place, that have been perfected and are just waiting for you, the innocent, unaware consumer, to come along. Unfortunately, these days trying to get a square, fair deal from many service providers is like trying to safely get through a pack of hyenas with an animal carcass tied around your neck!

Companies form every industry have perfected ways to inflict their own brand of dirty tricks on their customers. According to a report by the National Economic Council (NEC) states that due to declining competition in the marketplace American consumers are spending more and more on hidden fees. The NEC wrote. "At their worst, such fees can be fraudulent or deceptive; at a minimum, they make prices unclear, hinder effective consumer decision making, and dull the competitive process." These fees work to at least $942 in extra charges for every adult in the US!

The following list merely scratches the surface of shameless tricksters:

Cable and internet companies

I hardly even know where to with these horrible, greedy corporations! If you are like most people you have a love hate relationship with your cable company. We love the convenience of the set-top box but hate the outrageous monthly fee to keep that darn box! We end up having to pay for a gazillion channels just, so we get the 3 we watch. What a racket! Another thing that many internet service providers get people with is when they up sell you on the speed of your service, the megabits per second (Mbps). A report last summer from the Federal Communication Commission found that 80% of broadband users only require, at most, 4 Mbps. Don't pay for something you're not going to use.

Your service provider will try to convince you that you need up to 20 Mbps. The cost of the upgrade in speed can be as much as 67% of what you are paying for the lower speed.

Anyway, the thing to watch out for with the cable company is all the fees that you will undoubtable encounter when signing an agreement. They'll advertise a package at say, $60 a month, but once they have added taxes and fees your monthly payment could be close to $80. Another thing they do is entice you with an introductory rate that lasts for the first few months then inflate it well above the initial rate. Watch out for early termination fees. Most of the time they will charge you a set amount for each of the months that are left on contract. I know when I wanted out my contract I had to pay I believe $30 for each of the 5 months that remaining on my contract. Finally, there is the extra monthly "rental" fees for equipment like:

- **The router**

- **Set-top boxes**

- **DVRs...**

To reiterate, watch out for:

- **Hidden taxes and fees in the small print. Better yet ask your sales rep about them and get your answer in writing.**

- **Expiring special introductory pricing.**

- **Early termination fees.**

- **Reoccurring monthly rental fees.**

- **Auto mechanics**

If you're like me finding a good, honest, and reliable auto mechanic has been one my life's most welcome accomplishments. They are few things as frustrating and stressful as being at the mercy of someone you have no confidence or trust in. There are horror stories everywhere about how a dirty mechanic or a crooked service chain has ripped off an uncountable number of people.

One of the most egregious charges people commonly see on a repair invoice is a charge for "shop supplies". They are charging you for thing like shop rags and lubricants. That's like going out to nice restaurant and being charged extra for the napkin and silverware! Dealerships often recommend services that you really don't need like fluid flushes and the replacement of parts that are not mentioned in the service manual. If you operate your vehicle like 95% of the population does you don't need to do it. You're probably already aware that taking your car to the dealer is going to cost you more than if you go to a mom and pop. Unfortunately, sometimes the service that you need done requires the expertise of a dealer mechanic, but often you will not.

Some common scams to watch for:

- **The dirty air filter**

    This is one of the most popular rip-offs. The mechanic tells you your air filter is filthy, and he show a filter that black with dirt. The scam is that they sometimes save old filters to show the unsuspecting to convince then to take the bait. Another thing about the air filter is which one is he talking about? The one that keeps debris out of the engine and working parts or the one that filters the air that circulates throughout the cabin. If it's the latter just know that that filter should last 15,000 to 20,000 miles and keep good records, so you know is the engine filter is due to be replaced.

- **The bad break scams**

  Many times, "bad" breaks just need new brake pads, turning and/or cleaning of the rotors. This is a low-cost repair. Sometimes the mechanic will try to scare you into changing out everything. The pads, rotors, calipers ...the whole none yards, even if you don't need it.

- **The oil change scam**

  Here is where they try to upgrade you to a more expensive that your car doesn't necessarily need or require. They try to sell you "premium" or synthetic oil by telling your car needs it and the technician cannot use a "lower" grade without your approval. They'll ask you to sign off on the work while talking up some technical issue in the attempt to coerce you into the more expensive products.

- **Faking a leak**

  A truly dirty trick! A bad shop will spray coolant somewhere on the engine and then point it out to you to get you to repair or replace your radiator. Make sur you have the mechanic show you exactly where the leak is when contemplating this type of repair.

- **Unauthorized repairs**

  If a shop does work to your car without prior authorization from you and demands payment, provided it was completely unrelated to the original problem, you may be able to sue the mechanic.

Making unnecessary repairs or failing to put in the proper part(s) would also fall under the category of unauthorized repairs. If the shop made a good faith effort to solve a problem and fixed something else along the way, perhaps as a possible solution to the original problem, paying for the car repair work may be the best move. This is especially true for older models.

- **Contractors**

Hiring a contractor is serious business. Hire the wrong one and you could have a catastrophe on your hands. The following are some things for you to aware of, so you can avoid missteps that could cause grief and aggravation as well as end up costing you more than you had expected.

- **Bad bids**

If you receive a bid that is way less than others you have previously received double check to make certain that the bid covers everything that other, competing bids included.

- **Agreeing on quality**

Be sure you know exactly what quality materials you'll be getting. The grade of products can vary widely so you want to make sure that you and your contractor are on the same page when it comes to materials.

- **Inflated prices**

Contractors sometimes inflate the prices for people they

believe have deeper pockets. Living in certain areas and having a high paying career can make you a target.

- **Paying up front**

  Not all contractors are going to be the best business men. Sometimes contractors do not keep separate accounts on their clients. Small companies are the most vulnerable to this problem. They could end up using your some of your deposit to finish work on someone else's project. Then be expecting to use money from a different job to complete your project. I'm sure you can see how this could become a problem. I'm not saying that they would intentionally mislead you or be trying to defraud you but we all know things happen that are beyond our control all the time. Your contractor is certainly not immune to life's little bumps. You just want to be confident that your contractor is keeping your money earmarked for your job.

- **The have the right license**

  Do they have a business license and a contractor's license? Different states will have different licensing requirements. In Virginia for instance there are class A, B, and C licenses. Each class is attained after a certain number of hours worked and level of expertise reached.

- **Delays**

The classic contractor problem. Contractor's often under estimate the length of time a job is going to take. Many times, they are running small businesses with lean staffs and because of that they can easily get behind schedule.

- **Banks**

  Everyone today who has a bank account or credit card surly already knows the pain of being in the stranglehold of these financial giants. Make a mistake brother and it's going to cost you bigtime!

  According to a recent report by the *Pew Charitable Trusts' Safe Checking in the Electronic Age project*, the ten biggest banks disclose an average of 49 fees on their websites, but there are many hidden fees mostly involving account overdrafts. They recommend that the new Consumer Financial Protection Bureau require banks to offer customers a one-page fee disclose box, like the credit card companies already do. Hey, it's a start!

Some fees that you should have a clear understanding to avoid any nasty surprises are:

- **Account overdrafts**

- **Cash advances**

- **Stop-payment**

- **Balance transfer**

- **Payments made over the phone**

- **Lost card replacements**

- **ATM fees**

- **Account minimums…**

These are just a sampling of the fees the banks constantly squeeze out of their customers. Shoot, one of my accounts, an "e account", does not even allow me to go the drive through or a walk-up teller without them charging me for the privilege of speaking to a real person!

- **The hotel industry**

    The hotel industry adds mandatory 'resort fees' to customer bills on top of the advertised price. These fees equal $2.04 billion dollars. That is a whopping 16.6% of the industries revenue.

Then there are some more nefarious scams that an unsuspecting guest could fall victim to:

- **The fake flyer**

Before calling a number on a flyer you found in or around the hotel lobby make sure the business is legitimate. Scammers have been known to print up fake restaurant flyers and place them around hotels in order to dupe people into giving up their credit card numbers. The unsuspecting tired traveler decides that having a quick meal delivered to the room is just the break they need and calls in to order a pizza. The pizza never comes becomes there is no restaurant. They dirty tricksters now have your credit card number and can do whatever they please with it.

- **Wi-Fi skimming**

This is something that everyone who uses free public wi-fi access need to be aware of. A scammer can set-up year own Wi-Fi hotspot in a hotel, park, restaurant, or other public area. Once you start using the connection anything you send over the network goes directly to the scammer and they have all your information. Any username and passwords can now be used by them to infiltrate your accounts.

- **Fake call from the front desk**

If you receive a phone call from the front desk telling you that there is a problem processing your credit card information and they need you repeat the information red flags should go up. If this does happen be sure to go in person to the desk and give your information face-to-face with the hotel employee.

- **Entertainment**

Service fees on things like concerts and sporting events added to more than $1.6 billion in 2015 alone. Even though there is very little you can do about this I felt that because this is egregious it had to mentioned along with all the other rip-offs in this section! I guess you could say this is a personal rant!

- **Mobile and land-line phone service**

According to one estimate, most Americans are paying $300 more a year than they should for cell phone service. In recent years companies have raised overage fees, directory assistance charges and internet access. A practice called 'cramming' has cost consumers at least $2 billion since the 90s. Cramming is when the cell phone company charges for services they don't yet offer and allow third-party companies to attach costs. A report about cramming says that often "customers do not know these services have been set up for them and the mobile phone companies are unlikely to make the process clear to the consumer because they make money from them.

Land line phone plans have added fees like 'regulatory cost recovery fee' and 'administrative fees' as well as other fees with names that just as vague. All these fees are paid to the phone company even it sounds like the money is going somewhere else. It's all smoke and mirrors!

- **Home warranties**

I have personal experience with home warranties and do have coverage for some aspects of my home. I decided to purchase the warranties after years of seeing the same types of problems arising repeatedly. I have an issue with a tree that keeps clogging my sewer main and my refrigerator's original warranty has just expired, and I have had to have the icemaker worked twice in the warranty period. Because I know these things are likely to happen again I went ahead with the warranties. The warranties I do have already more than paid for themselves. But, that is not always going to be the case. Everyone's situation and needs will be different.

Every year there are thousands of consumer complaints filed against warranty providers with the Better Business Bureau. Obviously, a lot of other people have not had the same experience as myself. The lesson here is research any company you are considering doing business with before you purchase the warranty. Check for complaints about denial of service, exclusions, and any guaranty of repair from time of complaint. If your plumbing is out you sure don't want to have to wait three days for service!

- **Airlines**

One of the worst, the airline industries fees raise more than 22.5 billion dollars with things like baggage and change fees! Fees for things like rebooking a flight and checking your bag are one of the most obnoxious on this list. There are also things like rigged baggage scales to watch out for.

If possible it's a good idea to weigh your baggage before you get to the airport for two reasons:

- You'll know exactly how much they weigh

- Therefore, you know how much you'll have to pay

I understand that it is a hassle but if can weigh you bags yourself ahead of time you know for sure that what they are charging you for is legitimate. You could stop at the at a grocery store that has one of those giant scales and get the bag's weight. Easy peasy! Also, another thing you should do is make sure that the scale they are using is set to 0 before the attendant puts your bag on it.

- **Appliance repair**

  What a nightmare this can be. This is almost as bad as the tricks and deceitful practices that are found in the automotive industry. Some nasties:

- **Give me that money, I'll get the part**

  Never hand over money until the work is complete. If the repair person asks you to pay upfront, you have the wrong repair person. If you do this, you have left yourself wide open to be ripped off. They could easily take off with your money and you never see them again.

- **Leaving the repair person alone in the house**

  This unfortunately, is something that everyone should be concerned about. If you are like me, you tend to trust. I was taught to give people the benefit of the doubt. This attitude could be a big mistake when dealing with a repair personal (as well as other

people!). When a dishonest service person is confident that you are not paying attention, you leave yourself open to all kinds of dirty tricks. They have carte blanche. They could lie to you about what repair work was done and what parts they replaced. Not only that if the repairman has a criminal mindset you could even experience losses of a more personal nature. What if they decided it was safe to check out your jewelry box or go through your dresser drawers? They could even raid your medicine cabinets for prescription medications. How violated and stupid would you feel then?

- **Lying about licenses**

  Did you really look at their licenses? It is so easy and even feels good to just take people at their word. Don't do it. Make sure that are licensed to do the *kind* of work you have hired them to do. There are many types of licenses. Make sure you have covered all the bases by verifying their credentials.

There are so many dirty tricks and scams that I could go on forever. I hope that the previous provides you with some great food-for-thought. My intention is not to have an exhaustive list but to get you motivated and begin thinking about things in ways that maybe in the past were foreign to you.

It is surely almost impossible to keep up with the ingenuity and slipperiness that scam artists embody. They're are hard at work every day, in every nook and cranny of the world coming up with ways to separate people from their money.

Some tried and true scams that I didn't go into are ones that are perpetrated over the phone and the internet. Some active and prolific frauds as of the writing of this list include:

- The IRS calling to collect past due taxes, or they are going to send the sheriff after you.

- A stranger calling and asking, "can you hear me?" When you answer "yes" they are recording your voice to use to authorize future charges.

- Charity scams. The people go after and manipulate by tugging at your heart strings. Be extra vigilant when making donations to new or unfamiliar charities.

- The "Consumer Protection Agency," scam. Someone calls claiming to be from the Consumer Protection Agency to inform you that you have won a huge sweepstakes from the Make-a-Wish Foundation. They tell you that you must first pay thousands of dollars to cover taxes or insurance on the prize. What makes this even harder to spot is that often the call will come from the Washington DC area code (202) to appear credible.

- Virus alert. A pop-up tells you that your computer is critically infected with a virous and you need to call such and such number to get it removed. They then get you to send them money for bogus anti-malware and virus removal. The only thing removed is your money!

As you can see the list goes on and on!

Ten: Stay Organized with Great Records!

This section is probably the most important one in this whole project. You must have great records and reminders in place, keep up-to-date notes and have a working model that helps you to keep track of all the accounts you are juggling. If you fail at this your whole strategy is at risk. You must check and recheck all the balls in the air to keep your strategy in motion and working as planned. I can't stress this enough! Without a good recordkeeping system, your whole financial plan can, and most likely will, completely fall apart and backfire, doing more harm to your financial life than the good that will come from working this plan.

So much of this system relies on time sensitive accounting. Miss one deadline or expiration date and you could undo months', or even years, worth of effort and progress.

You must be on-point when keeping track of special terms and introductory offers. After all, those fabulous introductory offers will eventually expire and then the account could become a dog and turn around to bite you. You could now see a higher interest rate and/or additional fees.

The best way to tackle this project is to start at the beginning, of course.

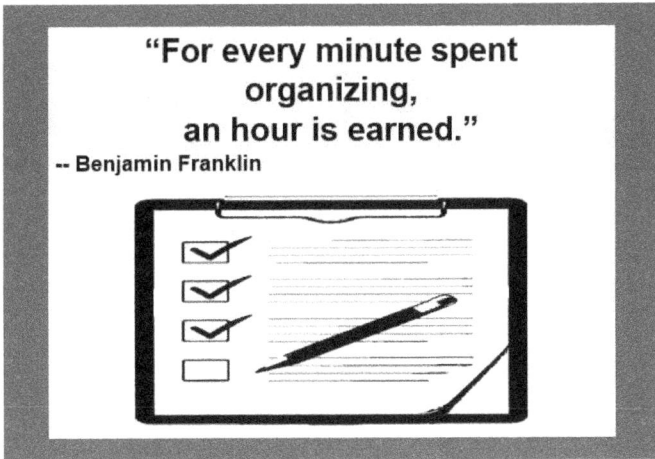

"For every minute spent organizing, an hour is earned."
-- Benjamin Franklin

1. **Take your inventory**.

Get all your credit cards together. Create a 7-column table with as many rows as you will need to list all the cards and back accounts you already have. Include the following information in the table:

a. The card/account name

b. The card/account number

c. The card/account issuing bank

d. The date the account was opened

e. The card/account perks

f. For perk cards list the best purchases to make with the card

g. Include some notes like, what you need to do to keep the card open and/or what

h. If any interest rates an account is earning and any other useful information.

My 2017 Credit Card Portfolio

Card/Acct name	Card/Acct number	Issuing Bank	Open Date	Benefits	Use for	Notes
Quicksilver	---- ---- ---- 5521	Capital One	06/2016	1.5% back on all purchases	Non-grocery, non-gas purchases	0% Interest until Sept, 2018

You are including the date the card/accounts were opened so you don't accidently close and/or let a bank close an older card/account due to lack of use. I have learned the hard way that some creditors will close an account after it has been inactive foe a certain amount of time. Remember that older accounts help your credit score by extending your history farther into the past.

This is how you are going to determine the steps that follow. Now it is not necessary to do this on a computer. You can always draw a table out by hand. Just be sure to leave enough space for your notes. Just understand that this is the foundation to your organization. Complete and accurate information is essential.

I will fill out the first row as an example:

I'm sure you get the idea. Keep this in a place that is convenient. You'll want this to be readily available, so you can update you list as you open or close accounts.

Knowing exactly where you and having a hard record of everything in your credit/account portfolio guides you onto the next step.

2. Filling in the gaps.

Start on the Web. Look for cards and/or accounts that fill any of your unmet needs.

Let's say that you have $5,000 just sitting in a regular checking or savings account. Wouldn't it be so much smarter to put at least some of that money into an interest baring money market account or even a CD?

You might have determined that you and your family are spending a good deal of your disposable income eating out. If you don't have a card that is giving you the maximum amount of cash back return (some are as much as 5%!) for restaurant purchases, you'll want to find and open one!

Once you have received your new credit cards and have opened your new bank accounts you'll need to have a up a way to keep track of any perks and offers that have been included.

3. **Paperwork & Records**

First, don't forget to add them to your inventory sheet. Then I suggest that you take advantage of cloud storage. There is a lot of free cloud storage out there. These are some great solutions. The amount of free storage varies from one to the next. And no matter who you are, free is always in the budget! Visit the web sites to determine if the storage solution is right for your O.S. and platform (Mac, Linux, Windows).

- Degoo

- DropBox

- Google Drive

- hubiC

- IDrive

- MEGA

- pCloud

- Sync.com

- Windows OneDrive

As well as taking advantage of one or more of these free cloud storage options you should set up and use a free digital calendar.

There are only 2 core functions that you will need from a calendar application. It should:

1. Show your upcoming schedule

2. Remind you of important events (i.e.: deadlines and expiration dates)

The calendars that made this list are:

- **Easy to use:** Intuitive and fast. Not too many clicks to get it done.

- **Aesthetically pleasing:** Have an uncluttered user interface (UI) and allow you to customize the appearance of different types of events.

- **Available for multiple devices:** cross-platform that gives you access to your schedule on the web by mobile device and desktop too.

- **Customizable with many features:** For the serious scheduler, features, such as customizable views or integrations with task management apps makes it possible to get the most from your calendar.

Some calendars that will meet your needs are:

3. Google Calendar

4. Apple Calendar

5. Microsoft Outlook ($6.99 per/mo.)

6. Sunrise

7. Blotter (Mac, iOS, $9.99)

8. DigiCal (Andriod)

With digital these tools in place you will be able to set reminders to keep yourself on schedule and never miss an important deadline or event. You might even consider using a budgeting software program. Budgeting software helps you create and stick to a spending and budget plan and usually has other personal finance features for managing your money. There are countless websites to help you determine the best software for your needs. Just do a search for personal budgeting software.

GnuCash

Quicken

Moneydance

Moneyspire

You Need a
Budget

More traditional means of record keeping

Now, we all know someone who is not a big fan of the whole digital technology thing. That person may even be you. Let's go over some smart things you can do to keep on track in a much less techy way. These techniques also work well as a compliment to more digital means of record keeping.

It's good to have a designated space for your bill paying and credit hunting work. I find that a box or basket that hold all my supplies together in one spot is handy and convenient. There's nothing worse than sitting down to do a task that I am not crazy about to begin with only to find that my supplies are scattered all over the house. So, I keep a box beside my desk with all the tools I will need to complete the task. Things like:

- **address labels**

- **stamps**

- **envelopes**
- **post It notes**
- **pens**
- **highlighters**
- **paperclips**
- **stapler**
- **a calculator**
- **a letter opener**
- **a mail scale to determine correct postage**

I also have an accordion file nearby where I file last month's bills. At the end of the year I empty the accordion file and start all over again with the new year. I keep a larger filing bin with hanging dividers inside for records and paperwork that I am keeping for the long run.

And it's a great idea to invest in a paper shredder. I have a small shredder that fits right on top of the trash can so that once I am done with paperwork I can shred to keep my personal data out of the hands of any would be crooks!

I find that by setting a certain day of the week at a specific time to take care of my bills, file, schedule bills, payments and just refresh myself as to what's brewing works very well. With this system, I have hardly ever messed up and missed a deadline. I say hardly ever because I on occasion I have marked something as done, got distracted in the middle of doing it, and then not realize that I had not actually completed the task, so it never got done! Because of this, I never mark anything as completed until I have submitted, it if online, or addressed and stamped the envelope if manually.

Some other supplies you might consider investing in are stamps and ink pad. If that it would be a great time saver to have stamps with the phrases like, For Deposit Only, my name and address, paid by (with a date function), you can get them inexpensively enough at an office supply store.

I have put together a calendar that keeps me on track and helps me to keep on top of all the different things I am juggling at one time. With this I don't miss any deadlines or forget about any new offers that I have chosen to put aside to decide later whether to pursue them or not.

This is how I use my favorite organizing tools. I will start with the actual credit cards themselves. When I get a new card in the mail that is for a specific task I'll take a post it note and write down any information about the perks and specials that come with that card. What I am using the card for and the expiration date of each perk associated with that card. I will include any other pertinent info I feel needs to be remembered. I then attach that little sticky note right to the card. I then go into my Google account, pull up my calendar and scroll to about 3 weeks before the perk is going to end and set a reminder to email mail me on that date a few weeks before the offer ends. This way I have plenty of time to make other arrangements for how to handle whatever balance remains on that account. Sometimes I just pay it off, or if I have another great offer I can take advantage of I might just move the balance to that new offer. Then I just repeat the whole process again!

I have again used the banks money for free! Another win!!

The paper work that came with the card goes into my long-term file box under the credit card file. I write on the front of the envelope the date I got the card, what I am doing with the card, when the offer expires and if I have not used the card yet or not. I make note of the offer that came with the card and some ideas as to how I could use it in the future.

The cards themselves go into a small fire safe I keep in my house. All my credit cards are there with their sticky notes attached and held together with a rubber band.

I then put all my accounts into my online bill pay at my bank. Each account gets a nickname to help me remember what it is for and there is a small space for me to make notes on each one of my bill pay account. I use that space yet again remind myself about deadlines and expiration dates.

So, as you can see I now have not one, not two, not three, but four separate places that contain all the important information I need for each account.

I should mention the importance of user names and passwords. I know there are programs that people use to keep their user names and passwords under lock and key, but I have a simpler way to do it.

Once again, I am use a combination of technology and traditional record keeping strategies. I mentioned cloud storage earlier in this section and this is where it comes into play. I use it to keep that information easy to retrieve for reference and update. No matter what machine or mobile device I am using I can get to my information quickly and easily. Before I used this technique, I was writing stuff down and could never really keep up with any changes that were made. I used to get so frustrated when my usernames or passwords would not work. I just felt like spitting fire!

So now I have one Word document that contains all my user names and passwords. I keep this document buried inside a folder that is inside another folder that is again inside another folder that is stored in the cloud. Each of these folders is giving some obscure title that I think no one would have any interest in looking at. For instance, you could use a name like "Aunt Carol's 80th".

Is anyone really going to be interested in digging through a bunch of files to look at some old lady's 80th birthday party? I think not!

I also periodically email that same document to my email address and just let it sit either in my inbox or my files just, so I have another, back up copy, that I can refer to.

I do use this way of record keeping for all my commitments. Not just credit stuff. Taxes, insurance payments, HOA dues, whatever. This gives me a few weeks of extra cushion, so even before I get notice of an upcoming expense I am prepared to handle the bill.

Of course, not all my credit cards are stored in the fire safe. There are the ones that I keep in my wallet for every day purchases. Normally that is like 2 or 3 cards in my wallet at the most.

I do have one right now that pays me 3% back on each purchase every month and then at the end of the first year they are going to match that amount and give it to me a second time. This is my everything card. It happens to be Discover that is offering this great reward, but some places do not accept Discover and I want to ALWAYS get something back! So, I carry another card that is paying 2% on all purchases. I use it where they don't accept Discover. I have even put my reoccurring cable/internet bill on my Discover card, so I will get the 6% back on that too.

This really is easy and works well. I believe that once you start doing all the things we have talked about in this program you will end up just like me. You will be so excited about all possible ways that you can "beat them at their own game!" that you will become as addicted to this as I am.

Free Money Now! Action Calender

Dailey

Go through your mail every day and look for credit offers and bank issued convenience checks. Decide what to do. Accept the offer, shred it, or save for later.

Go through and read or delete mail in your email accounts.

If you get a lot of email you'll want to check your Spam box a few times a week for offers and notices that may have been unintentionally thrown out.

Weekly

Set up auto payments from checking/savings through your on-line banking or set up reoccurring payments directly to the vender with your highest rewards cards.

Make sure that previously scheduled payments have gone through.

Look at any "save for later" snail mail. Decide if you can now use or feed it to the shredder, or should you wait longer to decide.

Monthly

Carefully review all your bank statements for mistakes or unauthorized payments.

Get your free credit score and see what's happening. (I like CreditKarma.com)

Review your notes and make any offer expirations or new offers to take advantage of.

Make sure ALL of your credit accounts are paid on-time! One late payment could mess up a good thing.

Quarterly

Evaluate plans and projects for effectiveness and make any needed adjustments.

Take inventory. If you see anything that needs to be done begin planning to get it done. Get your cards lined up, open new ones if necessary.

Review the banks policy for any paid off accounts and make a small purchase if necessary to keep a card open and alive. (Keep your combined limits as high as possible for the benefit of your scores!)

*Yearly: Get your free credit @ annualcreditreport.com

®www.freemoneynow.info

Finally, for those of you who do not feel that you have the time or have gained enough understanding to work this system there is always the Credit Management professionals that we discussed in chapter 3. There a lot of options and I'm certain everyone can find a good agency close to home.

Third party management of your credit cards:

Though a lot of people are comfortable with going forward with credit card debt management all by themselves, not everyone is. There are people who don't really want to tread into the territory of financial issues (credit card debt management included). However, even before we talk further on this topic of credit card debt management, it's imperative to understand that any external person or agency can only do a proper credit card debt management for you if you strictly follow the advice/guidelines that they formulate as part of credit card debt management. These credit card debt management guidelines are generally related to controlling your spending (which basically means perseverance and contentment). A person would probably be most interested in this type of service if they have gotten off track and found themselves in a financial bind. My hope for you is that you are just the opposite of this and are happily winning the financial game.

Going to a credit card debt management company or a credit card debt management advisor/professional is not meant only for people who are foreign to financial topics but is sometimes fruitful for other people too (who are going with credit card debt management all by themselves). This arises from the fact that these credit card debt management professionals (as any professional) would have more knowledge in that field than anyone else that is not from that field/profession. Firstly, you wouldn't know all the tips and tricks that the credit card debt management professional would know (and in fact this is something that you cannot read and learn overnight). And secondly, it will save you a lot of time because the person who practices credit card debt management as a profession will know about all the latest offers etc. that are available in the market (e.g. balance transfer offers etc. and hence you don't need to go looking for all this stuff all by yourself). Overall, a credit card debt management professional can help get you a better deal that might more than compensate for the fee charged by that professional. If you look around you will find that there are hordes of companies and professionals offering credit card debt management services. However, the key here is that you choose someone whose credentials are already established (or who can prove his credentials to you). One good way of selecting a credit card debt management company/ professional is to check with a friend or someone from your family, if they have used any such service in recent times. After all, references are the best way of building trust.

I want to take this opportunity to just remind you again about how vitally important it is that you master the things found in this chapter.

Even if the processes in this chapter seem foreign to you, after doing the steps for a few months I'm sure they will soon become just another part of your daily routine and not require too much extra effort.

Eleven: The Long Haul – Now What?

You are well on your way to winning the game and using other people's money to finance your life!

I will use this last section to look at and address some final miscellaneous items that we have not yet discussed.

Keep your cards and papers safe

You will want to make sure that you have a good secure place to keep all your credit cards, convenience checks and loan paperwork. I did mention before that I use a small locking fire safe to keep all my cards accessible and secure. Now, if I had any worries of robbery or other misdeeds that could be perpetrated upon me I'm not so sure that this would be my first choice for storing my body of work, so to speak. Other ideas for keeping your cards safe is a safe deposit box at the bank. You could even keep them in a storage room off property if you happen to already have one. There is a foolproof way to make sure that no one can get their hands on a card and that is to destroy it!

If you have one specific purpose for a card and it has done its job why not just close the account and get rid of the card? I'm not suggesting that you do this with all your cards because you do want to keep your usage to total credit below 30 percent and closing old accounts is a mistake. This would only apply to new accounts.

Tracking new offers

Checking out your daily mail was only briefly mentioned before so it seems like something worth bringing up again.

You will see that the farther you get into this plan you will begin receiving more and more offers from credit card companies and lenders soliciting you for business. Take a few minutes every day to sit down at your designated work spot and quickly sort through everything you received that day. Place your bills in your letter file and give a quick scan over any other offers that cam that day. If you can decide right away about the status of the offer great, if not that's okay too. You'll just want to make sure to shred anything that you have decided against so that no one can raid your trash and get those unwanted financial documents in their hot little hands! Someone could do a lot of damage with credit card conveyance checks if they were so inclined!

If there are some offers you are just not sure about make sure that you file them in a place where they will still get your attention and not be forgotten.

Clue the kids in

Us grown-ups are not the only ones who benefit in some lessons in how to smartly use money and handle credit. Think about it. One day the kids will right where you are. Wouldn't it be a huge blessing to already know what to do and what not to do *before* bad decisions and the consequences that come with them have a chance to happen?

It seems obvious that you wouldn't worry young children with money issues but there are some things that you should be sharing with your children about money from as early as 3 to 5 years old. This is a good time to start giving them pretend money (some even have play credit cards!) or a toy cash register to begin familiarizing them with the use of money. It is also an appropriate time for you to introduce them to concept of work for pay. Tell them about your job and explain that by doing your job you can pay for things like the house they live in and the food they eat. You could even explain to them what the coins in your pocket are, and how many pennies and nickels equal a quarter and so on. Just give them some idea as to the value of money.

When they are a little older, like elementary school age you can get a little more technical in your talks and activities. This is also the right time to start giving an allowance. It has been suggested that age 5 is a good time to begin giving an allowance. Talk to them about spending and encourage them to save for bigger purchases. Help them set a goal and encourage them to keep saving until they reach it. Take advantage of shopping trips. Use them for educational purposes.

Let your 5 – 8-year-old be the "chef" and decide on menu items for dinner some night. Take them with you to the store and let them collect the items and pay for them at the cash register. There is no better way to learn than to do. (It's also a perfect opportunity to introduce them the art of fine dining!)

By the time your kids are in middle and high school you should be approaching the subjects of credit cards, car loans, mortgages, and such. It's a good time to talk about the processes involved in buying big ticket items and negotiating terms. It is also a good time to think about opening them a checking account. Let them use their debt card to make purchases on-line and at brick and motor stores, the gas stations, wherever. Tell them about your car buying experiences and what you went through to get approved for your mortgage. They need to hear about the consequences of defaulting on a loan or missing a credit card payment. Late fees, bounced checks, credit denials are all a part of life, and they need to be prepared.

Hopefully by the time your kids reach college age they have a great understanding of the responsibilities of being a good steward over their finances. They handle their first credit card responsibly and are not tempted to run up unnecessary debt with student loans they could really do without. A recent Capital One poll found that 87 percent of 12 – 17 - year-olds reported knowing at least an average amount about managing finances, but of them 24 percent believed that a debit card was used to borrow money. So apparently, they are not as enlightened as they think they are. It's your job to make sure that they have a healthy respect for the power of money and credit

About college aged kids and credit cards. Because so many teens were got into trouble using credit cards congress passed, and then then-President Barak Obama signed into law, the 2009 Credit Card Act which raised the legal age for getting a credit to 21. That means if your kid is to have a credit card they will have to be an authorized user on your card, or you can co-sign for them to have their own card.

Just make sure that they really get how important it is to handle their money and credit wisely.

About co-signing.

When you have good credit (scores between 700- and above) it is easier and less expensive for you to buy a home, lease a car or get other kinds of credit. It also could make you a magnet to others who do not have good credit.

A study by the Federal Trade Commission found that 75 percent of sponsoring cosigners end up paying off, at least part of, the loan themselves. Creditors even go after the person with the strongest credit first, even before the primary holder!

There are a few important things to consider *before* you cosign anything. Whether it be a credit card for your kid, a car loan for you best friend or even a mortgage for a trusted relative take the time to educate yourself first.

- You will be equally responsible for the loan as the primary applicant. Anything that results from the loan will appear on your credit report. All terms must be completely clear to you and the person you are cosigning for. You don't want to get into the middle of a situation like this and find there were some details that were not discussed.

- Since you have the stronger credit you should be the one to set the tone for the agreement. You set the rules, make sure the co-signee knows all your expectations going into the arrangement.

- Understand that even the most trustworthy person you know can stumble and t

leave you holding the bag. Consider things like the health of person and their job security. Be prepared to, if it becomes necessary, repay the loan yourself.

Manage your risk by:

- Knowing the co-signee well
- Reviewing your own budget for validation that you can comfortable pick of the slack if the deal goes south.

- Get copies of everything. You need to know exactly what's in those papers you singed.
- If you can get out of the position of cosigner, do it. If the co-signee has an opportunity to refinance without your name encourage them to do it. ASAP!

The bottom line is that cosigning on anything is risky at best, and grave at worst.

Enter with extreme caution!

Now, Get Going!

Congratulations! You have reached to finish line! Now you know exactly what to do to get your financial affairs moving in the right direction! Some final thoughts:

- Do not get discouraged! Keep those inspirational juices flowing. You may need to occasionally remind yourself that this is going to take some time, don't let doubts convince you that this transformation is not going to happen. I know for sure that it is just a matter of time before you find yourself moving happily down the path to financial security.

- Do not forget how critical your record keeping system is to this process. It is so important to stay on top of everything you've got going on. Any falters could ruin your well-made plans! Customize your method wherever you can and just do what works for you. My way is my way, it works great for me. But you may find that you have a system that is completely different from mine that suits *your* journey better than anything I have suggested.

- Finally, it's a really good idea to put some thought into the accounts you are considering closing *before* you close them. Remember that this is a double-edged sword. Although it is beneficial to close used up promotional accounts, so you are once again a candidate for special offers. At the same time, you don't want to hurt your score by lowering your total available credit by too much at one time.

And last, but unequivocally not least, I want everyone to know that I am fantastically humbled knowing that in sharing my obsession with those who suffer financial bondage I am helping them to finally find peace and serenity! I cannot imagine a greater reward! That is without a doubt, the very best part of "Beating them at their own Game!"

Works cited

Kossman, Sienna. "2015 Cash Advance Survey: Convenient cash will cost you plenty." CreditCards.com. Creditcards.com, 02 Feb. 2016. Web. 18 July 2017.

www.ingramcontent.com/pod-product-compliance
Lightning Source LLC
Chambersburg PA
CBHW031941190326
41519CB00007B/606